Waiting For My Water To Break

How To Give Birth To Your God Designed Destiny

Dr. Tobias Everett LaGrone, D. Min.

Dr. Tobias E. LaGrone(tobiaslagrone@gmail.com)

ISBN: 1974338991
ISBN-13: 978-1974338993

DEDICATION

I dedicate this book in memory of the woman who birthed me into this world, the late Mrs. Margaret Dean Fields LaGrone. She taught me how to love, laugh, live and hope beyond my present circumstances. At the age of 32 years old she was diagnosed with breast cancer and she fought this disease for five years with dignity, faith and grace. At the age of 37 years old God called her home to her eternal reward. Thank you, mom, for inspiring me, Reginald and Tasha to always keep our hope in God's ability to do the miraculous.

I dedicate this book in memory of my two grandmothers, Mrs. Queenie Fields Harris and Mrs. Hannah Sisks LaGrone. Mama Queen, thank you for being a mother to the motherless and for allowing your house to be that place where any weary soul could call home. Mama Hannah, thank you for being that soft voice of reason and quiet strength when our lives seemed to be falling apart. Thank you both for taking me to Sunday school, Church Services, praying for me, and for helping me to develop my personal relationship with Jesus Christ. Thank you both for believing in me, investing in me, and pushing me to become who I am designed and destined to be! I hope I have made you proud!

Thank you, Mrs. Mary LaGrone, for breathing life and hope back into my father's life. Thank you for making our family whole again. You are our rainbow after the storm! Mother Mary, we love you more than words can say!

FOREWORD

Dr. LaGrone is a longtime colleague and mentor. We share in common our love for Christ and the spiritual gifts of exaltation which are manifested through psychotherapy. Dr. LaGrone is well respected and versed in the field of psychotherapy. He offer's specializations in the areas of mindfulness and its application to pastoral counseling. He has a gentle heart and keen understanding of the psychological needs of women. This book is right on time and is exactly what is required for Christian women preparing for both physical and spiritual pregnancy. After reading this book, I instantly knew the importance of this book and its divine purpose to touch the lives of millions of women.

Anyone dealing with fertility challenges recognizes it can be an emotional and lonely experience. From my personal experience, I understand the moments when you question yourself, and I dare say; moments when you may question GOD Himself. This book is invigorating in that it examines your deepest darkest secrets through the lens of biblical scripture. After reading this book, you will realize you are not alone. God has been in the business of healing brokenness for thousands of years. Dr. LaGrone uses traditional stories of the Bible and presents them in a new light in which they become applicable to those in various phases of motherhood.

You will learn to seek God at the well! Drop the water pot of carrying past burdens and shame! Gain confidence to avoid forfeiting your divine destiny! You will find joy and peace of mind in your situation! Most importantly, you will be able to give God praise!

Dr. Janique Washington-Walker, Ph.D., Clinical Director and Therapist at Strategic Paths Counseling Center

FOREWORD

Dr. Tobias LaGrone has once again delivered a timeless and masterful body of writing that will surely inspire, motivate, and encourage all who read it. At a time in his life where time is surely of the essence, Dr. LaGrone has generously poured his heart and soul into this work. The thoughtfulness of the specific biblical figures he uses is relatable to any reader, no matter their age, race, socioeconomic status, or profession. The practical analogies that he uses to deliver messages of purpose, faith, truth, and hope, will undeniably empower each and every reader to reach their God-given destiny!

Dr. LaGrone has unselfishly given us a road map and guide to understanding God's divine purpose for our lives. At a time when all seems lost in this world, this "fresh oil" reassures us that God is with us, always! I am humbled to call Dr. LaGrone my friend and brother. I am grateful that God has used him to encourage the masses through his writings. I have watched him grow over the years, and his personal pain and triumphs bleed through in every word of this anointed work. As I read this book, I literally got chills because I knew it was personal. It left me with a renewed sense of purpose. As you read, my prayer is that you experience what I felt and more. Be blessed.

Ms. Kelli N. Singleton, M.S., United States Probation Officer at Federal Judiciary

Special thanks to my book cover model
SYDNEY ELAINE MACON

Special thanks to my book cover photographer
REV. RODERICK CHARLES of *HIS WILL PHOTOGRAPHY*

FIRST PRINT / FIRST EDITION

CONTENTS

	Acknowledgments	10
1	Pregnant With Purpose	12
2	God Is Changing My Appetite	20
3	Pregnant Purpose at A Dry Well	33
4	Don't Abort Your Destiny	46
5	Refuse To Be Their B.I.T.C.H.	56
6	Giving Birth to Your Greater You	69
7	A Pre-Natal Praise	74
8	Wars In the Womb	84
9	Surviving the Pregnant Pause	105

ACKNOWLEDGMENTS

I would like to thank the love of my life, Mrs. Patricia Wade Freeman LaGrone, thank you for believing in the calling that God has upon my life. Thank you for trusting me enough to marry me at a young age and loving me enough to push me towards my God designed destiny. Thank you for not quitting, thank you for not allowing me to quit! I could not do what I do without your dedicated love, commitment and support. I am truly blessed to call you my wife of 25 years.

Thank you, mother-in-law, Dorothy Wade Freeman! Your quiet strength serves as a constant source of strength, hope and unconditional love for our family.

Last, but not least, I would like to thank my daughter, Tabrea Ann-Marie LaGrone, our child of brains, brilliance, and beauty. Tabrea you are a bright star of hope that past generations of our ancestors prayed for. God has anointed you to live a life that is reflective of His power, love, mercy and grace. You are the joy of my life!

1

Pregnant With Purpose

"There Is A 'Destiny Seed' Inside of You"

In the physical it takes only a few minutes for a man and woman to co-mingle and thereby initiate the process of pregnancy, and what only took a few minutes to start now takes a long, lengthy nine months to come to fruition.

Normal pregnancy is divided into three segments called trimesters. The first trimester begins at conception and continues about 12 weeks of the pregnancy and at the end of the first trimester the fetus (baby) has a recognizable human form. Zechariah 4 states; [10] Do not despise these small beginnings, for the LORD rejoices to see the work begin, to see the plumb line in Zerubbabel's hand.

Out of the millions of sperm that were competing to fertilize your mother's egg, you are the one who made it through. You are already a champion! You are already a winner! You are on the road to obtaining your God designed destiny whereas you will finally feel and look like the winner that you already are. Zechariah 4: 10 a-b: [10] Do not despise these small beginnings, for the LORD rejoices to see the work begin.

Every created thing had a small beginning, look at the oak tree in St. Mark 4:[30] Then Jesus said, "How can I show you what the kingdom of God is like? What story can I use to explain it? [31] The kingdom of God is like a mustard seed, the smallest seed you plant in the ground. [32] But when planted, this seed grows and becomes the largest of all garden plants. It produces large branches, and the wild birds can make nests in its shade." ***(NCV)***

God has planted a destiny seed of purpose within each and every person. This seed of faith is the key to us identifying and locking into the reason and purpose for which God allowed us to be born. Satan, that enemy of all that is holy, right, and true comes as a wild devouring beast to eat up our seeds of faith in order to divert us from our God designed destiny.

Jesus Christ said in the parable of the sower in St. Matthew 13: [18] "Hear then the parable of the sower: [19] The seed sown on the path is the one who hears the word of the kingdom without understanding it, and the evil one comes and steals away what was sown in his heart.[20] The seed sown on rocky ground is the one who hears the word and receives it at once with joy. [21] But he has no root and lasts only for a time. When some tribulation or persecution comes because of the word, he immediately falls away. [22] The seed sown among thorns is the one who hears the word, but then worldly anxiety and the lure of riches choke the word, and it bears no fruit. [23] But the seed sown on rich soil is the one who hears the word and understands it, who indeed bears fruit and yields a hundred or sixty or thirtyfold."

The rich soil is the fertile ground of one's inner faith; faith is the fertilizer of the soul. One must allow the word of God to cultivate the ground of one's mind, soul, and spirit thereby providing a fertile, faith-full, nutrient rich soil for one's destiny seed to grow and produce the God designed destiny that God has inside of that person.

Satan is the seed snatcher, the one who comes to steal our hope, dreams, and God designed destiny. The seed which ended up in rich soil produced more results than any of the other seeds. One fourth of the seed fell by the wayside and the birds (scavengers) came and ate them up, one fourth of the seed fell in a rocky place which had no soil and when the seed blossomed it withered because it had no soil for its roots, one fourth of the seed fell among thorns and wild brier and when they blossomed they were choked and overshadowed by the wild growth. Only one fourth of the seed landed in good soil and yet because of this **seed being in the 'destiny will' of God,** this seed produced thirty times, sixty times, and one hundred times what it normally should have produced. At minimum, the seed that fell on good ground, **destiny ground**, produced 180,000 times what the whole field was supposed to produce in the natural. When we rest in the destiny will of God our life is guaranteed to produce an abundant harvest of super-natural proportions.

Joseph did not have sexual intercourse with Mary until after Jesus the Messiah was born. Jesus Christ, the Messiah, is the only begotten Son of the true and living God and his conception and birth was a sacred event. The Virgin Mary, the mother of Jesus was a pure virgin who had not been touched with the sin of fornication.

When God chose the Virgin Mary to be the human vessel to give birth to the Son of God, God was in essence recreating a human form of His divine self by inserting His God-Self into the human condition through the sacred womb of a virgin woman.

Sexual intercourse is a sacred act; it is not something that should be perceived as nasty, disgusting or evil. Sexual intercourse is ordained by God in order for man and woman to be able to duplicate God's presence in the earth. When a man and woman engage in sexual intercourse the man and woman become lost in each other. They are sealing the binding contract of marriage and literally inter-mingling and exchanging the most intimate parts of themselves with each other.

When the husband inserts his sexual organ into his virgin

bride, he literally breaks the hymen, the biological and spiritual seal of the woman's virginity that covers his wife's sexual organ. The blood that is produced as a result of this sacred seal being broken by the woman's husband, symbolizes a blood covenant that is sealed in the eyesight of God and the married couple. During the days of Jesus in the Mediterranean world, the husband would take the white sheets from the wedding bed and hang the sheets on the door post or yard fence, allowing all to see the blood-stained sheets, proving that he had married a virgin and the marriage covenant had been sealed by the intimate blood covenant of sexual intercourse.

Be Careful Who You Sleep With

Each time you open your legs and allow a man to enter the sacred temple of your inner self, there is potential for a pregnancy to take place. You may be saying that you are pass the age of childbearing years, maybe you take some type of contraceptive medication, or maybe you have some type of birth control device implanted.

The type of pregnancy I am talking about is not a physical pregnancy but a spiritual pregnancy. It is important for you to understand that your life is a fertile womb, and you will become pregnant by people you allow to enter into the fertile womb of your mind and soul. If you surround yourself with people of hope, faith, and positive thinking then that is what will feed your faith and impregnate the womb of your mind and soul with life and unlimited possibilities. If you allow negative, critical, gossiping, lying people to enter the intimate spaces of your life you will be filled with negative energy that can not produce a healthy destiny.

Every person who smiles in your face is not coming into your life to be your friend; the devil sends some people to sabotage your destiny. The scriptures say in;

2 Corinthians 11:14-15 (HCSB); *14 And no wonder! For Satan disguises himself as an angel of light. 15 So it is no great thing if his servants also disguise themselves as servants of righteousness. Their destiny will be according to their works.*

The old saying is true, people are like elevators, some people can lift you up, some people can take you down, and some people can leave you stuck in between floors in a tight space with no way out! Make sure that you begin to guard your life more closely, this is important because negative energy gives birth to more negative energy and positive energy gives birth to more positive energy.

The Ovaries of Potential

The woman's menstrual cycle is the monthly series of changes a woman's body goes through in preparation for the possibility of pregnancy. Each month, one of the ovaries releases an egg through the process called ovulation. At the same time, hormonal changes in the woman's body prepares the uterus for pregnancy. If ovulation takes place and the egg hasn't been fertilized by the male sperm, then the lining of the uterus sheds off through the vagina, which results in what is described as the menstrual period.

When God allowed you to be constructed and formed in your mother's womb, God placed within you the ovaries of potential. This means that you are not an accident, you being born is not a haphazard event. You may have been a surprise to your parents, but you were never a surprise to God. God spoke you into existence when God determined which one of the sperms from the millions of sperms your father released into your mother would ultimately connect with your mother's egg.

You are a unique soul! You are one of a kind, unique and special in your own way. You were born a unique original therefore it would be a sin for you to live your life as cheap copy imitating someone else! There is no one anywhere on earth with the unique qualities that you have. When you were conceived in your mother's womb God downloaded 'destiny software' into the hard drive of your psyche and soul, this 'destiny software' has preprogrammed you to be the answer to somebody's problem. You are preprogrammed with everything you need to live a prosperous, successful and fulfilling life. God affirms this truth in the book of **Jeremiah 29:11 (NKJV);** **"**11 For I know the thoughts that I **think** toward you, says the LORD, thoughts of peace and not of evil, to give you a future and a hope." The Hebrew word for **think** in this passage is **chashab**, which means to plan, to devise, to calculate, to interpenetrate and weave together. God is literally saying that when He created you, He already had in mind where He would weave you into the scheme of life on planet earth. God has already devised a plan for you to make significant contributions during your lifetime.

God has already calculated when, where, and how your unique set of gifts, talents, and 'destiny calling' will contribute to making life better for others and bring glory to the Kingdom of God.

God is saying that He will interpenetrate you into the grand play of life, therefore you don't have to adopt a dog eat dog mentality, you don't have to be a cut throat rat racer trying to get ahead in life, all God asks you to do is to be your own unique God designed self and at the right time God will open the doors for your success.

2

GOD IS CHANGING MY APPETITE

Now that it has been confirmed that you are definitely pregnant, you are now beginning to understand why you have been having morning sickness. In the early stages of pregnancy, the woman begins to experience nausea and times of vomiting. The woman's stomach is upset because a disturbance is taking place within her, the body knows that changes are occurring, and the body is preparing to adapt to the 'new normal'. The body is readjusting itself in order to provide the forming embryo with all the nutrition and cellular support that is needed in order for a developing fetus to form into a healthy baby.

In addition to your morning sickness, you are having strange cravings for different types of foods, your sensory perception has become heightened, and you can smell food from a mile away. Foods you ordinarily loved to eat are of no interest to you, now you are craving strange combinations of food, like eggs and mayonnaise sandwiches, peanut butter on cinnamon toast, or smoked salmon with potato soup.

Your pregnancy is causing your desires to change. You are craving something out of the ordinary and outside of the box. When you come to the spiritual awareness that God has impregnated you with the purpose of divine destiny, the appetite of your spiritual consciousness will begin to change! You will no longer want to consume the same old drama filled conversations from gossipers. You will stop allowing negative people to enter into your personal space. You will lose your appetite for those things that are not pleasing to God and are also unhealthy for your social, emotional, professional and spiritual growth.

God wants our appetite to be drawn towards the fruits of the Spirit. Galatians 5:16-25 (ASV); 16 But I say, walk by the Spirit, and ye shall not fulfill the lust of the flesh. 17 For the flesh lusteth against the Spirit, and the Spirit against the flesh; for these are contrary the one to the other; that ye may not do the things that ye would. 18 But if ye are led by the Spirit, ye are not under the law. 19 Now the works of the flesh are manifest, which are these: fornication, uncleanness, lasciviousness, 20 idolatry, sorcery, enmities, strife, jealousies, wraths, factions, divisions, parties, 21 envyings, drunkenness, revellings, and such like; of which I forewarn you, even as I did forewarn you, that they who practice such things shall not inherit the kingdom of God. 22 **But the fruit**

of the Spirit is love, joy, peace, longsuffering, kindness, goodness, faithfulness, 23 meekness, self-control; against such there is no law. 24 And they that are of Christ Jesus have crucified the flesh with the passions and the lusts thereof. 25 If we live by the Spirit, by the Spirit let us also walk.

When we fail to live by the leading of the Holy Spirit, our carnal appetites are drawn towards the things in life that are not pleasing to God, nor are they beneficial to our well-being.

When my family and I walk through the food court of the local shopping center, the local restaurant establishments have employees standing there passing out free samples of sesame, teriyaki, and honey barbeque chicken hoping to entice us into buying their product. If the bright sign didn't lure us in, if the smell didn't entice us to partake, then the offer of the free sample was sure to seal the deal. The sample taste of the product stirs your 'appetite' by tantalizing your taste buds. The sample of the taste causes the flesh to wake up and want more.

Where is your mental appetite? What do you want out of life? What do you want your life to look like this time next year? Take a mental inventory of what you spend the most of your time doing and who you spend your time with, and this will give you a preview of where your life is going. Are you engaging in activities that will make you a more conscious thinker? Are you reading rewarding books? Are you sharpening your professional skills in preparation for starting your own business or applying for a promotion at work?

Doctors instruct some expecting mothers that there are some foods they need to avoid because of their pregnancy. This doesn't mean that the foods are not good or offer some nutritional benefits, but the restriction implies that these particular foods may be good for others, but not for you, because you are pregnant.

There are some people, places, and things that were common and acceptable in your life before your pregnancy, but now that you are expecting, it is time for you to change some people, places and things in your life. God wants your expectations to change! God wants your psychology of success to grow to the point where you stop being bothered by what people think about you; you make your top priority to be more concerned about what God desires to do in your life.

Jesus Christ engages His disciple Peter in an epic dialogue regarding the importance of self awareness and spiritual growth in this particular passage of scripture.
Matthew 16:13-23 (ASV); 13 Now when Jesus came into
the parts of Caesarea Philippi, he asked his disciples,
saying, Who do men say that the Son of man is? 14 And
they said, Some *say* John the Baptist; some, Elijah; and
others, Jeremiah, or one of the prophets. 15 He saith unto
them, But who say ye that I am? 16 And Simon Peter

answered and said, Thou art the Christ, the Son of the living God. [17] And Jesus answered and said unto him, Blessed art thou, Simon Bar-jonah: for flesh and blood hath not revealed it unto thee, but my Father who is in heaven. [18] And I also say unto thee, that thou art Peter, and upon this rock I will build my church; and the gates of Hades shall not prevail against it. [19] I will give unto thee the keys of the kingdom of heaven: and whatsoever thou shalt bind on earth shall be bound in heaven; and whatsoever thou shalt loose on earth shall be loosed in heaven. [20] Then charged he the disciples that they should tell no man that he was the Christ. [21] From that time began Jesus to show unto his disciples, that he must go unto Jerusalem, and suffer many things of the elders and chief priests and scribes, and be killed, and the third day be raised up. [22] And Peter took him, and began to rebuke him, saying, Be it far from thee, Lord: this shall never be unto thee. [23] But he turned, and said unto Peter, Get thee behind me, Satan: thou art a stumbling-block unto me: for thou mindest not the things of God, but the things of men.

Peter was accurate in his spiritual discernment and description of who Jesus was, Jesus is indeed the only Begotten Son of the one true and living God. Peter got it right and as a result of Peter getting it right, Jesus confirmed that Peter would be His chief disciple and apostle to lead the church once Jesus has returned to heaven, but the positive mood soon turns sour without notice. When Jesus began to tell His disciples that He would suffer many afflictions and ultimately be crucified and die a horrific atoning death upon a Roman cross Peter became enraged and defensive.

Verse 22 of this reading says that Peter took Jesus by the arm and began to rebuke Jesus, telling Jesus to stop talking like that because Peter was willing to fight until the end to protect Jesus. Now Jesus was forced to rebuke the same Peter he had just bragged on! How is it that within a matter of minutes, Jesus compliments Peter, appoints Peter as the head of God's church and within the same conversational engagement he now tells Peter; "Get thee behind me Satan?"

When Jesus confronts Peter with the words; *get thee behind me Satan*, Jesus is not speaking to the Personage, Persona, or the outer layer of Peter's physical self, but Jesus is speaking to the 'Person Peter', the True Self of Peter whom Satan is trying to entice with power, position, and prestige of this world. Jesus is educating both Peter and us in a psycho-spiritual methodology that the outer appearance that we present to others is merely our Persona or Personage, ***'the me I want others to see'!*** Yet within the deep recesses of each person lives 'a True Self, a real Person, an authentic Self' which is designed by God to seek out the perfect will of God, but sometimes we allow our flesh, our emotional self to get in the way of God's perfect will for our life.

Jesus' rebuke of Peter had to be a major blow to Peter's ego and self esteem: 'Get thee behind me Satan'; well maybe Peter's inflated ego was just what Jesus was aiming to hit. Jesus had to remind the human side of Peter, the fleshly emotional side of Peter; that you are not in control of God's plan for my destiny. As well intentioned as Peter may have been in showing his love and concern for Jesus, even Jesus refused to get in the way of God's plans.

Jesus was trying to communicate to Peter that Peter's focus had turned to the wrong thing, Peter's spirit had answered correctly that Jesus is the Son of God, but Peter's emotional self, the flesh driven self, wanted Jesus to set up an earthly kingdom and rule the earth with Peter and the other disciples by His side. Jesus called Peter a stumbling block who was attempting to trip Jesus up and prevent Jesus from accomplishing God's destiny plan for Jesus' life. The word stumbling block is translated in the Greek language to ***skandalon***. This word is best described in the English language as being a **trap stick.**

When I was little boy, my grandfather taught me how to trap a rabbit, he would take a heavy wooden box, prop it up with a wooden stick, tie a string to the wooden stick and place a little grain under the box. The rabbit's appetite only saw the enticing grain and failed to notice the trap stick that was holding up the wooden box that would trap the rabbit. Jesus was telling Peter that Peter only sees the enticing grain of sitting on a throne ruling the earth with the Son of God, but Jesus sees the trap stick and wooden box of pride that would prevent Jesus from giving His life as a living sacrifice to save us from our sins and eternal damnation.

Jesus was telling Peter and us as well, to change our appetites, to get our minds off of the things of this world and our own selfish desires, and to yield our life to the perfect will of God the Father! Peter had envisioned an earthly government where Rome's imperialistic power would be overthrown, and the reign, rule, and righteousness of God would reign on earth, but Jesus professed that His Kingdom is not of this world! Jesus professed, St. John 14: [1]Let not your heart be troubled: ye believe in God, believe also in me. [2]In my Father's house are many mansions: if it were not so, I would have told you. I go to prepare a place for you. [3]And if I go and prepare a place for you, I will come again, and receive you unto myself; that where I am, there ye may be also.

God knew that Peter's person, Peter's true inner self determined what Peter's real appetite was. God knows that our true person, our true inner self determines what our real appetites are. God knows that there are some secrets we hide in our true self, some sinful things our appetite craves in private that we shun in public; some secret sins we indulge in private that we will not be seen near in public. The danger is not the fact that all of us are wrestling within our Person, our true inner self; the gravest danger is not knowing who you are and what lies beneath the surface of your persona and outer facade. If you don't know what it is about your psycho-spiritual diet that the devil keeps trying to feed you, to snare you and entangle you, then you don't know what you need to diet from, fast from, and ultimately take out of your eating habits all together.

Jesus Christ is challenging Peter to allow God to change his appetite whereas Peter stop savoring and craving the things of the flesh and seek after the deeper things of God. God wants us to develop such a spiritual hunger for the things of God, to desire an intimacy with Jesus Christ where we hide nothing from Him, where we place 'Our All' on the alter and cry out like the Psalmist, Psalm 42: *As the deer pants for the water brooks, So pants my soul for You, O God.* [2]*My soul thirsts for God, for the living God.*

Morning Sickness and Mourning Sickness

When you experience the awakening that tells you that there is more in you than you are allowing to come out, then you begin to evaluate your life and began to make the necessary adjustments that are needed in order for you to move to the next level in life. When you realize that you are pregnant with unlimited potential you begin to take inventory of who you have in our life, and you ask yourself the question; is this person a helper or is this person a hinderer? Is this person an asset or a liability? Is this person helping me to climb higher or is this person dragging me down? When your spiritual eyes are open by the power of the Holy Spirit, then you will go through what I can best describe as mourning sickness.

Just as a newly pregnant woman goes through 'm-o-r-n-i-n-g' sickness, a newly aware child of God goes through 'm-o-u-r-n-i-n-g' sickness, this means there will be a period of time in the life of the newly aware believer when he/she will realize that they have to separate themselves from those who are not a positive influence on their faith development. The mourning takes place because this is a period of time when you are separating from the old, negative, familiar people of your past and trusting God to connect you with positive, faith-filled people who will motivate you to be-come your destiny self.

During the early stages of pregnancy, the woman goes through a series of screenings; she experiences medical tests that look for genetic diseases, vitamin deficiencies, and other possible biological health hazards to the growing child. Doctors may advise certain lifestyle changes which may cause the mother to give up something that she really likes, this is the consequence of pregnancy; sacrifices have to be made in order for a healthy child to be birthed. Sacrifices have to be made in order for you to be-come your destiny self!

The process of pregnancy is a long nine-month progression that culminates with a beautiful child being born, but the whole ordeal can be challenging. In the

Book of St. Mark 4:[26] Jesus also said, "Here is another illustration of what the Kingdom of God is like: A farmer planted seeds in a field, [27] and then he went on with his other activities. As the days went by, the seeds sprouted and grew without the farmer's help, [28] because the earth produces crops on its own. First a leaf blade pushes through, then the heads of wheat are formed, and finally the grain ripens. [29] And as soon as the grain is ready, the farmer comes and harvests it with a sickle."

Sometimes while we are waiting for our time of harvest and breakthrough to manifest itself, we become worried, despondent, and depressed. What we must realize is that even though it may take a long time for the seed of our destiny purpose to manifest itself, while our seed of destiny is covered under the dark, fertile soil of our faith, we must always remember that there is a difference between being ***buried*** and being ***planted***. God has planted the seed of destiny in you, so even though it feels like your God designed destiny will never come to pass, remain strong in the hope of your faith. God has not buried you; God has planted you! Hang in there because soon your mourning sickness will turn into morning joy and gladness. The Psalmist proclaimed in **Psalm 30:5 (NKJV);** [5] For His anger *is but for* a moment, His favor *is for* life; Weeping may endure for a night, But joy *comes* in the morning.

Jesus tells us what we are going to see in our life when we remain connected to Him and committed to God's destiny design for our life; the seed produces a blade. The leaf blade pushes through the resistance of the dark earth. The leaf blade pushes through the very thing that has had it covered and has been placing pressure upon it. Without the covering of the earth and its nutrient rich surroundings the seed would not have had the surroundings it needed to produce. The earth provided the proper environment for the hard outer husk of the seed to decay and expose what is in the seed to that which surrounds it and further prompts the seed to soak in what it needs and use those surroundings to make it strong enough to break through its surroundings.

The heads of the wheat form above the earth showing that the seed in the earth has manifested the great potential that was always locked up inside of it from the beginning. The head of wheat is a manifestation of the potential that was locked inside the seed, yet would have remained dormant and unlocked until the seed was placed into its God designed environment, the earth.

When the head of grain ripens then it is ready for the harvest. The word ripens means that the seed has reached a level of maturity and wisdom whereas the seed is now ready to walk in the power of its harvest. The ripen grain which came from one seed has now produced thousands of cornels of grain. You are about to come into your harvest and the God designed destiny that is locked up inside of you is getting ready to bring forth a great harvest, both for you and those whom God has assigned to be blessed by you and through you! Get ready for the Harvest! God didn't allow you to be placed in the dark and damp environment that you are presently in order to bury you; God is using the circumstances of your present situation to plant you in the fertile soil of faith which will cause your seed of hope to germinate and break through the barriers that currently have you bound.

3

PREGNANT PURPOSE AT A DRY WELL

Here we encounter Jesus embarking on a special assignment to encounter a nameless woman living in a shameful condition. This Samaritan woman is identified by her issue, an issue that is beyond her control, an issue of being born within the geographical bounds of the territorial region of Samaria. The woman's lot in life had already been predefined by others who felt that for various reasons they were better than her, more holy than her, and more worthy of life, love, and liberty that she could or should ever be.

Have you ever felt trapped by your life; trapped by where you were born; trapped by who you were born to; trapped by the circumstances you were born into, trapped by what you decided to do; trapped by who you decided to do it with or trapped by opportunities you allowed to pass by your way? This woman was trapped by circumstances beyond her control, but when she encountered Jesus at the well, she encountered the living water of God in the person of Jesus Christ.

Samaria could be a lonely place. The word Samaria means watch tower, a place where those who lived there were always looking for something more. In order to get something more in life, you must begin to look for something more.

Samaria is the place that Jesus says He must go through! Jesus is going through a place that other people avoid in order **to empower a woman** with whom nobody else wants to be bothered. I am glad that Jesus doesn't mind going out of His way to find us at the place of our brokenness, searching and longing.

When Jesus arrived in Samaria, He went to the village of Sychar. This word is translated to mean the drunken place. This woman is living in a drunken place, a place that intoxicates its inhabitants with the belief that this place is all there is to their life. The lie of Sychar says you were born here and you will die here. Sychar are also those wounded emotional places in our life that discourage us from trying to reach for more in life. Sychar offers the intoxicating drinks of discouragement, depression, and defeat, but Jesus is coming to our rescue with the life giving water of hope and destiny.

Jesus encounters the woman in **John 4:7-9 (ESV);** [7] A woman from Samaria came to draw water. Jesus said to her, "Give me a drink."[8] (For his disciples had gone away into the city to buy food.) [9] The Samaritan woman said to him, "How is it that you, a Jew, ask for a drink from me, a woman of Samaria?" (For Jews have no dealings with Samaritans).

Jesus asks the woman at the well for a drink of water,

and she rebukes his request by stating the obvious friction between Jews and Samaritans. Jesus was not detoured by this woman's hard out shell because He knew that at her core a 'destiny child' of purpose was waiting to break forth from the womb of destiny.

Jesus answered the woman and said, "If you knew the gift of God, and who it is that is saying to you, 'Give me a drink,' you would have asked me, and I would have given you living water." Sometimes we can allow the pain of past wounds to block us from the blessing that God is placing at our door. This woman was hard and abrasive with Jesus but he did not allow her emotional hurt to stop Him from seeing the value of her God designed destiny. Jesus was offering this woman living water, **living** *(**zao**-breathing)* **water** *(**hydro**-rivers, pools, reservoirs).* Jesus was trying to communicate to this woman, who was so stuck in the drunken place of a dead end existence, that she needed the **Holy Spirit**! The Greek word for Holy Spirit is paraklet, which means 'one who speaks in favor of you as an advocate, intercessor, comforter and counselor'.

John 4:11-12 (ESV); [11] The woman said to him, "Sir, you have nothing to draw water with, and the well is deep. Where do you get that living water? [12] Are you greater than our father Jacob? He gave us the well and drank from it himself, as did his sons and his livestock." It is here that this Samaritan Woman begins to move from a mere surface level casual dialogue with Jesus and begins to engage Him in an interpersonal psycho-spiritual self analysis. In verse 11 the woman said to Jesus, "Sir *(Kyrios-master/owner)*, you have nothing to draw with, and the well *(phrear)* is deep!" The ancient word for *well* that she uses here in verse 11 is different from how the word *well* has been used previously in this chapter. Earlier in this chapter in verse 6, the Greek word for well is *pege*, which means fountain or spring, is used to refer to a physical well that is dug in the ground.

In verse 11 when the Samaritan Woman says; "*Sir, you have nothing to draw water from this well with, and the well is deep!*" She uses the ancient word phrear which means abyss; dark place, a hell that gets deeper and wider the further it goes down! This woman is attempting to warn Jesus that if he isn't the real thing, then He should turn around and leave her alone before He falls into the deep, dark, abyss of her living hell. She is warning Jesus that many men have come into her life. They were attracted to her body, but they couldn't handle the pain of her past.

She is warning Jesus, this 'man' who has met her at this well, that He needs to be careful before He starts digging around in her life, because the deeper He goes, the messier her life gets. The deeper He goes the darker her life gets! She is warning this man, Jesus, that she has met other men and most of them made promises that they couldn't keep. They started off good, but when they dug down into the pain of who she was and the horror of what she had been through, one by one they left her high and dry! Now she is trying to size Jesus up to see if He is for real, or is he just like the other players that ran in and out of her life. She wants to know if Jesus is interested in her, or is he just trying to get at her body. Before she becomes vulnerable and allow Jesus into the secrets of her heart, she needs to know if He is just playing games with her.

GIVE ME THAT WATER

John 4:15 (ESV); [15] The woman said to him, "Sir, give me this water, so that I will not be thirsty or have to come here to draw water."

This woman was tired of coming to the well to get the water she needed on a daily basis. She came at the hottest part of the day because she wanted to avoid the crowd. She wanted to avoid other women who came to the well in the late part of the day when the temperature was cooler. She came at the hottest part of the day in order to avoid encountering other women, married women, honorable women who reminded her of her dishonorable way of life.

Jesus meets this woman at the well of her wanting. She had less, but she wanted more. She was asking for physical water to cool her tongue, but deep down within her SOUL she was crying out; "Please God, let this man Jesus have what I need to quench the thirst of my dry SOUL!"

Jesus is offering this woman freedom from the bondage of her dry situation, but her freedom comes at the cost of her learning to be truthful. She asks Jesus to give her the water He is talking about. Jesus is willing to give her the water of life freely, but she must pay the shipping and handling cost with the debit card of TRUTH! Jesus said; **John 4:16 (HCSB);** [16] "Go call your husband," He told her, "and come back here."

The woman told Jesus she didn't have a husband! She was trying to manipulate Jesus into believing that she really didn't have a husband because she didn't want to face the 'TRUTH' about her 'SELF'. Jesus asked her to go and call her husband as a test to whether or not she was ready to deal with the truth about her own life. Jesus called her out and revealed the facts of her life to her, revealing that Jesus already knew that she had actually had five husbands in her lifetime, and the man she has now is not her husband!

This should have been a sign to her that Jesus was more concerned about her as person, more than He was concerned about the religious legality of her immoral behavior. Jesus already knew the dysfunction of her life, yet He still went out of His way to track down this woman in order to change her life.

Jesus knew that she was either living with a man she was not married to, or she was involved in a romantic relationship with somebody else's husband. These are the factors surrounding this woman's self-shame, public humiliation, and inner emotional conflicts. Jesus did not come to judge her choices. He was there to liberate her life. Jesus' focus was on setting her free to grow and become her authentic God-designed self, but she was too busy trying to hide in the shadow of self deceit. Jesus can set her free, but her freedom comes at the cost of her finding the courage to be honest with herself.

Don't Change the Subject When Jesus Is Talking

She tried to do the same thing many of us do when we are confronted with some of the uncomfortable truths about our life. We try to change the subject or we try to start an argument. She attempts to move the conversation away from her personal life, and she attempts to start a debate about religion. She tried to turn Jesus' attention away from dealing with her issue; and she tried to start an argument about where she and other Samaritans worship; and where Jesus and other Jews are suppose to worship. **John 4:19-20 (NKJV);** [19]
The woman said to Him, "Sir, I perceive that You are a
prophet. [20] Our fathers worshiped on this mountain, and
you *Jews* say that in Jerusalem is the place where one
ought to worship."

The woman at the well uses a psychological defense mechanism called projective identification, whereas she falsely attributes her own unacceptable feeling to Jesus. While doing this, she remains aware of her conflicted feelings, yet she believes they are justifiable reactions, all while trying to divert the conversation from her and the mental disruptions that are caused when Jesus exposes herself to HER SELF.

She attempts to talk about the conflict between the Jews and the Samaritans in order to get the attention off of 'HER SELF', but Jesus keeps the attention right where it should be, on her! Jesus helps her to break free from both societal and self imposed limitations that are preventing her from growing into her God designed, self-actualized self.

Jesus doesn't fall for the bait and start arguing about where is the proper place to worship. Instead Jesus once again deals with the intra-personal being of this woman's inner self, by redirecting the conversation back to the subject of her being **'TRUTHFUL'**; truthful with God and most importantly, truthful with her inner self.

Jesus said; **John 4:21-24 (NKJV);**21 Jesus said to her, "Woman, believe Me, the hour is coming when you will neither on this mountain, nor in Jerusalem, worship the Father. 22 You worship what you do not know; we know what we worship, for salvation is of the Jews. 23 But the hour is coming, and now is, when the true worshipers will worship the Father in spirit and truth; for the Father is seeking such to worship Him. 24 God *is* Spirit, and those who worship Him must worship in spirit and truth."

To worship God literally means to bow down, kiss and

lick the hand of God because of your gratitude towards Him. To worship Him in Spirit and Truth means that you allow the Holy Spirit to fill you and flush out all Self Deceit, meaning you stop hiding from your Self!

To be truthful, in the Greek language, means to break free from all self deceit. You become totally honest and transparent with your own self and still choose to love your self because God loves you even though He already knows everything about you. Self love and Self acceptance is the catalyst for self change. You can not change anything about you until you first acknowledge that there is something in you that can be changed for the better.

Change in behavior happens after a change in Self Perception! If you can acknowledge that you can be better, then you can accept the challenge to become better. The Good News is that God loves us before we become better, but the best news is that our blessings are attached to us working to become better. Grace covers us while we are in the process of changing, yet the reward of greater blessings are not released to us until we make some necessary changes in our self and consequently, in our life.

Stop Allowing It To Hang Over Your Head

John 4:25-26 (NKJV); [25] The woman said to Him, "I know that Messiah is coming" (who is called Christ). "When He comes, He will tell us all things." [26] Jesus said

to her, "I who speak to you am *He.*" **John 4:28-30
(NKJV);** 28 The woman then left her waterpot, went her
way into the city, and said to the men, 29 "Come, see a
Man who told me all things that I ever did. Could this be
the Christ?" 30 Then they went out of the city and came
to Him.

This woman, who was previously ashamed to encounter women before meeting Jesus Christ, is now empowered to use the unashamed truth of her life to lead men and women to Jesus Christ. This woman has grasped the lesson that Jesus taught her. She now understands that the circumstances of anyone's life can be used by God to help others become who God has destined and designed for them to be. The prerequisite for this great gift is true honesty with one's self about one's self.

When she became who God designed her to be, she was empowered to empower others to come to Jesus Christ. Jesus Christ is the power source who empowers us to become who we are destined and designed to become.

Your testimony, your life's story is worth telling, but have you come to acknowledge the truth about your story? Have you owned the truth about some of the poor choices you have made? Have you yet owned the truth about the poor choices others made for you which you had no control over? Have you owned the truth that who you are becoming, is more important than where you were born, and to whom you were born?

Have you owned 'your truth' or are you still blaming your parents, an absent father, an addicted mother, a cheating spouse, a hateful boss, or a back stabbing friend for you still being stuck in the shameful place of a dry well?

This woman left her water pot and ran into town, stood on the public square and proclaimed that she has meet the truth teller, the truth giver, and the True Savior, in the person of Jesus Christ. By her acknowledging the truth about her inner self, and the truth about who the Son of God is, she was freed to drop her water pot and run back to town. When you know the truth about yourself and the God you serve, you can't help but be set free. Jesus said; "you shall know the truth and the truth shall make you free!" She came to know the truth about her self and God's love for her, and this truth set her free!

Her encounter with Jesus Christ freed her to live in truth with God, meaning that she accepted the fact that God loved her regardless of her past. Jesus Christ knew her scandal, but still chose to love her to life and purpose.

Her encounter with Jesus Christ freed her to live in true relationship with herself and others. Jesus empowered her to drop the water pot of her shame and to confront the people of her town. These are the same people she was too ashamed to even be in the presence of, not even daring to speak to them and certainly not daring to teach them about anything. She now realizes that they are no better than she is. She now realizes that the only opinions that matters in her life is her opinion and God's opinion.

The Woman at the Well can now testify; "Jesus sat on my well and made me drop my water pot. The water pot represents the emotional burden that drove me back to the place of my wounded well! My emotional well was suffocating the air supply of my hope and robbing me of my dreams. This external well had handcuffed the healthy inner emotional growth of my inner self and caused me to live in an incarcerated state of mental anguish; but Jesus Christ sat on the well of my dried up self esteem and caused a spring of purpose driven water to baptize my mind and spirit with the Holy Spirit. Now I have been empowered to 'flow' in the rhythm of life with purpose and power."

Drop Your Pot So You Can Run

The water pot, that all important tool for any person living in that culture, became unimportant when compared to the life giving power of the Holy Spirit that Jesus gave to her. Women carried their water pots on their heads. They balanced the weight of the pot and the water on their heads. With each step that the woman would take, she had to compensate for the weight of the water pot, in order to perfectly balance what she was carrying on their head.

The water pot becomes symbolic of the shame that was

always hanging over her head; the shame of having many husbands, many lovers and the shame of having both public and private sins. Are you ready to drop your water pot? Are you ready to stop having to make continuous psychological calculations about how you are going to walk through life, while struggling to hide those shameful things that you allow life to hold over your head?

Jesus Christ says you can become filled with the living water of the Holy Spirit, and drop your water pot of regret, bitterness, and pain. Jesus Christ proclaims that what is in you is more powerful than what others may have on you, or what may be hanging over you.

4

DON'T ABORT YOUR DESTINY

Naomi and her husband Elimelech left Bethlehem and went to Moab in search of a better life. There was a famine in their homeland of Bethlehem Judah, and Ruth's husband was not willing to wait on God to show him how to survive the famine. Elimelech failed to realize what so many of us fail to realize, that is, where God guides, God provides. If God allowed the famine to come, then God had already designed a 'famine proof' plan for those who trust in God.

Elimelech allowed the circumstances that surrounded him to push him out of his God designed place. Elimelech and his wife, Naomi, lived in the land Bethlehem Judah, literally meaning that they lived in the place of bread and provision (Bethlehem), and the place of God be praised (Judah). Elimelech moved his family to the country of Moab. The origins of Moab began when Lots' daughters got him drunk and engaged in incestuous sex with their father, Lot. Moab came to be known in a spiritual sense, as a place where people's decisions were led by the flesh and not by the Spirit of

God.

Elimelech's name means "my God is King", yet when it came time to trust God at the most critical time of Elimelech's life, he allowed his perceived needs of immediate survival to take precedence over God's destiny plan for his life. Be careful when you chose a partner, because their faith or lack of faith will have a direct effect on your destiny. ***What or Who you become tied to, can either lift you like a kite, or weigh you down like an anchor!***

Instead of toughing it out in Bethlehem Judah, the place of destiny, Elimelech and Naomi settled in Moab. Not only did they settle in Moab in a physical sense, they settled for Moab in a spiritual sense. The word "settle" indicates a psychological adoption of one's way of thinking, an acceptance and embracing of customs and ways of living. Sooner or later everyone becomes what they decide to settle for! What or who are you settling for?

Elimelech and his wife, Naomi, had two sons; and over the course of time, Naomi's husband died in Moab and Naomi's two sons died in Moab also. Naomi becomes a widow, and her two daughters-in-law become widows also. Elimelech led his wife into a dead end situation, or should I say Elimelech misled his wife into a dead end situation. Are your following a dude or your destiny? Are you following a person, a career, a golden opportunity, or are you willing to trust God and pursue your God designed destiny?

Naomi decides to return to her home in Bethlehem-Judah, and she convinced her daughter-in-law Orpah to remain in Moab; but Ruth, Naomi's other daughter-in-law, refused to be persuaded to remain in the land of Moab. Ruth wanted out of the mess she was born into. Ruth had determined that she has had enough of Moab and she was going to go to Bethlehem-Judah with Naomi. Even though Ruth is a grieving widow in a barren land, Ruth allows her hope to over power her grief.

The marriage covenant that we hear said at weddings between the bride and groom, was actually first said by a woman to another woman. When Naomi tried to persuade Ruth to stay in Moab while Naomi returned home to Bethlehem-Judah, Ruth said these words:

Ruth 1:16-17 (NLT); 16 But Ruth replied, "Don't ask me to leave you and turn back. Wherever you go, I will go; wherever you live, I will live. Your people will be my people, and your God will be my God. 17 Wherever you die, I will die, and there I will be buried. May the LORD punish me severely if I allow anything but death to separate us!"

The spirit of God moves Ruth to stretch her faith so she could dream beyond the barren, dry land she lived in. Ruth was ready to leave Moab and follow her destiny to Bethlehem-Judah. She is leaving the land of the flesh

(Moab) and going to the land where God provides bread (Bethlehem) and where God is praised (Judah).

Don't Become Bitter Because of Your Battles

When Naomi and Ruth arrive at Bethlehem-Judah, Naomi is greeted by the women of the city with a parade like atmosphere. Everyone is happy to see her, the whole town is bursting at the seams with joy. Everybody is rejoicing, except the guest of honor, Naomi.

Ruth 1:19-21(NLT);
19 So the two of them continued on their journey. When
they came to Bethlehem, the entire town was excited by
their arrival. "Is it really Naomi?" the women asked.
20"Don't call me Naomi," she responded. "Instead, call
me Mara, for the Almighty has made life very bitter for
me. 21 I went away full, but the LORD has brought me
home empty. Why call me Naomi when the LORD has
caused me to suffer, and the Almighty has sent such
tragedy upon me?"

Naomi has allowed her bitter battles to turn her bitter. Naomi's name literally means 'pleasant one' but because of what she has been through, she tells people not to call her **'pleasant one'** but to change her name to **'bitter one'**. Naomi is ready to abort her destiny because she feels like life has given her a raw deal.

Naomi is mad at God because she feels that God has not

treated her fairly. She has lost her husband and her two sons. Naomi is angry and she is confused as to why all of these disappointing things are happening in her life. Psychology informs us that anger is always a secondary emotion, meaning the emotion of anger can never come first. This emotion is always catalyzed or activated by a primary emotion of disappointment, fear, frustration, sadness, loneliness, etc.

Dr. Stephen Diamond, Ph.D., defines bitterness as "a chronic and pervasive state of smoldering resentment," and deservedly regards it as "one of the most destructive and toxic of human emotions."

Dr. Leon Seltzer contends that all bitterness starts out as hurt, and your emotional pain may well relate to viewing whomever or whatever *provoked* this hurt; generally, your assumed perpetrator, as having malicious intent: As committing a grave injustice toward you; as gratuitously wronging you and causing you grief. It is anger and its first cousin, resentment, is what we're all likely to experience whenever we conclude that another has seriously abused us. Left to fester, that righteous anger eventually becomes the corrosive ulcer that is bitterness. If we repeatedly ruminate over how we've been victimized, our "nursing" our wrongs may eventually come to define some essential part of *who we are.* Take hold of our very personality. And so we will end up becoming a victim, not so much of anyone else, but we end up becoming victims of our wounded self.

Naomi is professing that she has allowed her bitter circumstances to turn her into a bitter person. She has allowed her issue to possess her identity. We are encouraged by the writer of **Galatians 6:9 (KJV):** [9] And let us not be **weary**(ekkakeo = exhausted, utterly spiritless, worn out faith) in well doing: for in due season (God's timing) we shall reap, if we faint not.

Never allow the bitter circumstances of life to turn you bitter. Lemons can become lemonade when you take authority in the name of Jesus Christ and choose to squeeze the bitter lemons of your circumstances instead of allowing the bitter lemons of your circumstances to squeeze you.

Squeeze your bitter circumstances for all they are worth; your struggle may lead to a new invention; your problem may lead to a new equation for problem solving. The bitterness of darkness led to the invention of the candle, then the light bulb. The bitterness of long and tough travel led to the invention of the automobile and then the airplane. Every struggle has a destiny purpose and reason attached to it! I encourage you to squeeze out some lesson from your struggle; add the sugar of your faith, add the water of the Holy Spirit, and turn the bitter circumstance of your lemons into lemonade.

Your Answer Is With You

Yes, the answer to Naomi's problem was with her! Remember that Naomi had tried to persuade Ruth to return to her own family in Moab, but Ruth was determined to seek out a new path for her life. Little did Naomi know that Ruth was the key figure God was going to use to turn Naomi's life around, all while fulfilling God's ultimate purpose of giving Israel a new royal blood line.

God allowed circumstances to develop that brought Ruth into the presence of a wealthy distant cousin of Naomi's family. Boaz fell in love with Ruth, and Ruth loved him as well. After the appropriate customs of Boaz requesting that the Elders of the community grant him permission to marry Ruth, the two of them were married.

When Boaz and Ruth got married, not only did it change Ruth's life, but it changed Naomi's life as well. Both Naomi and Ruth instantly went from rags to riches, from being nearly homeless to now owning houses and land. God has a way of making our past pain pay present interest. In other words, God will give you double for your trouble.

If Naomi had of convinced Ruth to stay in Moab and return to her pagan family, Naomi would have forfeited the key that would unlock the door of her future blessing. In spite of the pain that Naomi experienced loosing her husband and two sons, and in spite of the pain that Ruth experienced losing her husband, God always had a greater plan in mind. God has a greater plan in mind for your life. God will not allow your pain to be wasted!

God has promised to bless you, but you must hold on to your faith in God's ability to bless you. Hold on to your belief that God desires to bless you! The devil tries to play tricks with our minds through the gateway of our emotions. The devil tries to convince us that God doesn't care enough for us to stop our pain or to stop painful things from occurring in our life.

I believe that God allows pain in order to get us prepared for the promises of His blessings. I appreciate, cherish and guard my blessings because of the pain I had to go through to get them. We guard that which is valuable! We guard that which we appreciate! Guard your blessings because nothing God gives is cheap.

Naomi allowed the pain in her life to psychologically cause her to lessen her own value. She took on the cheap title of 'bitter one', when God had already named her and valued her as being a 'pleasant one'. Stop allowing what you have been through in life to negatively label you and lower your expectations of what you feel like you deserve in life. Naomi had given up on hoping for a better tomorrow, but Ruth kept looking for more in life. Ruth kept her expectations alive. Ruth kept her hope alive. Ruth remained pregnant with faith!

Ruth 4:13-17 (HCSB); 13 Boaz took Ruth and she became his wife. When he was intimate with her, the LORD enabled her to conceive, and she gave birth to a

son. 14 Then the women said to Naomi, "Praise the
LORD, who has not left you without a family redeemer
today. May his name become well known in Israel. 15 He
will renew your life and sustain you in your old age.
Indeed, your daughter-in-law, who loves you and is
better to you than seven sons, has given birth to him."
16 Naomi took the child, placed him on her lap, and took
care of him. 17 The neighbor women said, "A son has
been born to Naomi," and they named him Obed. He
was the father of Jesse, the father of David.

Ruth gave birth to Obed. Obed would become the father to Jesse and Jesse would become the father of the great King David. It is through this great blood line that Jesus Christ would be born. Ruth gave birth, but the woman of the city said that a son has been born to Naomi. The woman said this because they understood that God had blessed Naomi with a complete turn around in her life.

Naomi's blessing, her daughter in-law Ruth, was with her all the time, but Naomi almost missed her miracle because she was stuck in the pain of her past. Your blessing is with you, if you just take the time to stop looking backwards and start looking around you. You are more than a conqueror, you are more than your past mistakes and failures, your are more than what people say about you.

Every struggle has given you a lesson! Every tear has taught you! Every set back has propelled you forward! You are right here, right now and your blessing is with you. Do you get it? Your blessing is with you! You are your blessing! You have life, strength and hope, as long as you have God's power working through you. Nothing is impossible if you have faith to believe!

5

REFUSE TO BE THEIR B.I.T.C.H.

One of the greatest threats to your professional development and personal success is who you decide to call your man, your lover, your boo, or your husband. God wants you to thrive in love, God wants everybody to have somebody to love and be loved by, however what God frowns upon is when you allow a significant other to become the 'god' in your life. God doesn't want you to surrender your God designed destiny to anybody, but this is what happens when you choose to settle for a man who doesn't respect nor promote your God-designed purpose and destiny.

When you find yourself dumbing down your conversation and suppressing your high level of intelligence just to keep him feeling secure, you are cheating yourself and lying to him because you are failing to challenge him to grow and become more. This is just one example of how beautiful, intelligent, high achieving, highly driven professional women like you allow yourself to become somebody's B.I.T.C.H. You settle for the wrong man, and in the process, you end up losing the 'true you' you were designed by God to become.

In the Bible **1 Samuel 1:1-8 (ESV);** 1 There was a certain
man of Ramathaim-zophim of the hill country of
Ephraim whose name was Elkanah the son of Jeroham,
son of Elihu, son of Tohu, son of Zuph, an Ephrathite. 2
He had two wives. The name of the one was Hannah,
and the name of the other, Peninnah. And Peninnah had
children, but Hannah had no children. 3 Now this man
used to go up year by year from his city to worship and
to sacrifice to the LORD of hosts at Shiloh, where the
two sons of Eli, Hophni and Phinehas, were priests of
the LORD. 4 On the day when Elkanah sacrificed, he
would give portions to Peninnah his wife and to all her
sons and daughters. 5 But to Hannah he gave a double
portion, because he loved her, though the LORD had
closed her womb. 6 And her rival used to provoke her
grievously to irritate her, because the LORD ha closed
her womb. 7 So it went on year by year. As often as she
went up to the house of the LORD, she used to provoke
her. Therefore, Hannah wept and would not eat. 8 And
Elkanah, her husband, said to her, "Hannah, why do you
weep? And why do you not eat? And why is your heart
sad? Am I not more to you than ten sons?"

Hannah was married to a very prominent and well respected man named Elkanah. Elkanah was married to Hannah and Peninnah at the same time, as was the norm during that time. Hannah was not able to have children and as a result, Elkanah's other wife Peninnah would agitate and aggravate Hannah by constantly reminding Hannah that she had no children. Elkanah loved Hannah and felt pity for Hannah because he knew how bad she wanted to have a child.

When it was time to go to the temple and worship, Elkanah would give Hannah a double portion of resources for temple sacrifice. One day Elkanah became frustrated with Hannah, he was watching her as she cried, mourned and refused to eat because she could not get pregnant. Out of frustration Elkanah asked Hannah; "Why are you crying? Why don't eat something? Why are you so sad? Don't I treat you better than ten sons could treat you if you had them?

Even though Elkanah was a good and noble man he didn't understand the true cause of Hannah's pain. Elkanah thought her pain and grief was because of her inability to give him a son; that was a minor part, but not the core of her pain. The core of Hannah's pain was centered in the fact that she knew she was pregnant with purpose, spiritual purpose, divine purpose, destiny purpose. It was not about having Elkanah's baby; it was about giving birth to the purpose that God had locked inside of her. This may be one of the reasons why God made Hannah want so long to have a baby. God wanted the birth of Hannah's child to be about divine destiny and not just about having a male child. Hannah's destiny desire fed her faith. Faith is the womb that incubates your God designed destiny dreams. In this instance I describe faith like this; **'Faith is the substance of dreams hoped for and the evidence of dreams not yet realized'**.

Just like Hannah, your destiny dream is the result of a destiny seed that God Himself planted in your psychological-spiritual D.N.A. while He was forming you in your mother's womb. Your destiny dream is fuel to drive your 'faith shaped imagination', whereas in spite of your present biological-sociological circumstances; you are inspired to reach beyond the doubts of your now, and use your faith shaped imagination to make your destiny dreams come true.

Hannah's destiny dream to give birth to Samuel was already embedded in the psychological-spiritual D.N.A. of her soul by the hand of God. Hannah was first impregnated in her spiritual psyche by the life giving breath (pneuma/spirit = psyche and mind) of God. It was her internal yearning that drove her emotional self to lament and struggle until her physical womb became pregnant with what her psychological-spiritual womb was already carrying.

The Bible makes it clear that Hannah was a worshipper! One particular time when Hannah was at the temple worshipping God with all of her heart, Hannah worshipped God with so much passion until the Priest Eli accused Hannah of being drunk. Hannah told Eli what she desired God to do for her, she wanted to conceive and give birth to son who she knew was meant to be a servant of the Lord.

After this divine worship experience, Hannah became pregnant, both Hannah and Elkanah were elated. Hannah named the child Samuel and she knew when he was old enough she would take Samuel back to the temple and dedicate him to God as temple priest. The deep passion and heart felt desire Hannah was feeling as she desired to give birth for all those years made sense when Samuel was born. Hannah was waiting for her water to break! Hannah was waiting for the manifestation of what God promised her to come to past. Hannah understood that she had to hold on to her faith that God was able and God would do it in God's own timing. Nothing happens without faith!

Hannah could have been content to just be married to a noble well respected man like Elkanah, he was wealthy and he loved her, but Hannah was not willing to exchange her destiny for wealth and prestige. Hannah was not like some of the woman today who are looking to marry a sugar daddy, a wealthy doctor, a famous actor or professional sports figure; Hannah knew that she had destiny purpose locked up inside of her and it was up to her to reach for her destiny purpose. When you decide to settle for comfort and convenience at the expense of forfeiting your God designed purpose and destiny, you are making the choice to become somebody's B.I.T.C.H.

God doesn't want you to be become anybody's

B.I.T.C.H. You owe it to God to become all of who you are destined and designed to be. Any human you surrender your destiny to becomes your god. You are not designed to only produce for someone else! You are designed by God to produce the priceless product of your purpose and purposes, for your own prosperity, and for the glory of God.

Those who own breeding dogs, meaning dogs they use to produce puppies in order to sell them, call the female mother dogs who produces the puppies bitches. The primary purpose of the bitch is to produce puppies that bring profit to everyone, except the bitch that actually births the puppies. The female dog, or bitch, produces for others, but she does not produce for herself.

I have counseled far too many women whose whole life has been about making others stronger, more successful, and more secure, yet after 20 years of pouring their whole life into a husband, children or a profession, one morning they wake up feeling broken, empty and lost. I am not suggesting that you become a selfish person who only looks out for yourself, no that is not what I am suggesting. I am informing you that if you give 'all' of you to your marriage, to your children, to your job, or even to your church, then what amount of energy, strength and spiritual fortitude will you have left to push out and give birth to the God designed purposes and destinies that God has impregnated you with?

Love your husband, love your children, love your

church, and have passion for your job, but don't turn them into idol gods. God wants you to practice good self care, God wants you to discover your own destiny identity while you are being a good wife, a loving mother, a faithful church member and a growing professional; yet God doesn't want you to get lost in the positions and titles you wear and you fail to become the greater you God has destined for you to be. Becoming your greater you is having a self-awareness of your inner being, an awareness that you are unconditionally loved by the God of the Universe! A God who wants you to continue to grow, blossom and live an 'on purpose life' until you breathe your last breath.

Husbands die, lovers leave, divorce sometimes happen, children grow up and move away, businesses close, careers change and churches sometimes forget your sacrifice. Yet when you know who you are and you continue to become, evolve and grow into your greater you, then no matter what life brings your way you are going to be just fine.

Who are you producing for? Who have you allowed to make you their B.I.T.C.H.? Is it your children, spouse, lover, family members, job, etc? God wants you to first produce for yourself and as a result, those who you love benefit from the overflow blessings of you producing and becoming who God created you to be.

B is for 'Blaming Bag'

There are some women who are in relationships where they are the one blamed for every negative thing that happens in her man's life. She allows herself to become the 'Blaming Bag'. Nothing she does is ever correct in his eyes, the chicken is fried to hard, the sheets are too soft, the house isn't clean enough, and she is never good enough. A man like this is dealing with his own intrapersonal psychological issues and he needs a blaming bag in order for him not to take a close look at his own short comings and insufficiencies.

You are driving yourself crazy trying to be perfect for an imperfect man when that is emotional energy God wants you to use to draw closer to God as you seek out your God designed purpose. Don't allow yourself to become somebody's blaming bag, because blaming bags soon become punching bags!

The blaming bag mentality is not limited to romantic relationships between spouses and significant others, the blaming bag mentality is also found in the parent child family dynamic. There are some parents who blame their child for the parent's failures. They will say things like; "If it had not of been for you, I could have had a successful life, or you are the reason our marriage fell apart, or you are just like your sorry mother, you are just like your no-good father." These types of blaming statements shift the responsibility for poor life choices from the responsible adult and place it on the shoulders of the helpless defenseless child.

Make up your mind to stop owning your parents' failures. You are not your father, you are not your mother, you are not your siblings; you are your own unique person and the only choices you are obligated to live by are the choices you make of your own free will and volition. You don't have to be anyone's 'blaming bag'.

I is for Insecurity

Emotionally insecure people perceive themselves to be inferior to others in some way and they compensate for this internal emotional feeling in various ways; one way they compensate is by attempting to make others feel bad about their self. They find slick and sly ways to belittle others; the insecure person wants you to be their cheerleader, applauding when he/she gets a promotion, gets a new car, house, or have some major achievement in life, but when it is your turn to be blessed and good things start to happen for you, the insecure person will always find something negative to say. They may make statements like; "Your new house is beautiful but the neighborhood is questionable. Your new car is cool but I would have gotten a newer model. Your promotion at work is good but how are you going to handle all of that new responsibility." There is always a 'but' attached to the compliment they appear to give you.

It is difficult to be in an emotionally healthy relationship with an insecure person because he or she will always look for a way to cut you down to the small size of his/her insecure mentality. If your man is insecure he will make statements that work against your self esteem, he will make statements that make you believe that nobody wants to be with you but him. Don't allow an emotionally insecure person to rob you of your God designed destiny. Don't be so desperate to be in a relationship that you surrender your God-designed potential.

If your intelligence and anointing causes those around you to feel insecure, that is their problem and not yours! You can not make a secure person feel insecure, only people who are insecure to begin with will show signs of insecurity. Don't allow someone to label you as the one to blame for their insecurities.

If you have children by a man other than the one you are with right now, then he must understand that your children need to have a relationship with their biological father as well. Don't allow your man's or husband's insecurities to cause to cut off communication from your children's biological father.

Don't allow someone else's insecurities to cause you to lessen your will and drive to reach for more in life. Don't be afraid to apply for the promotion at work, don't be afraid to get another college degree, don't be afraid to use correct English at home and with your extended family. Don't be afraid to be talked about by your family members who don't support your desire to break the status quo. You owe it to yourself to be all you can be!

T is for Triggers

Triggers are people, places and things that serve as catalysts which prompt an emotional reaction in a person. You may have heard someone say that they got angry because someone pushed their button, the button they are referring to is some type of psychological trigger point in their psyche. Don't allow anybody to blame you for their poor behavior. This is the excuse that exists in most domestic violence incidents, the abuser tells the abused; "See what you made me do to you!" These are poor excuses for poor behavior.

C is for Character

Character is defined as the mental and moral qualities of a person. The true essence of who a person really is. One's character is who they really are when no one is looking. Character must be an important quality in choosing a person to be in relationship with. Once again, don't compromise your integrity by settling for a person who has questionable character.

A person with questionable character will eventually influence your character over a period of time. I have talked to women who were hard working, stable, and making their way through life making the best out of what they had, then a man comes along who says all the right things but the woman knew that his behavior didn't match his words. Maya Angelo is the one who said; 'When a person shows you who they are, believe them.' Stop making excuses for his poor behavior, stop risking your future for his latest get rich quick scheme.

H is for Hindrances

Ask yourself the question, will my relationship with this man hinder my future goals and dreams? Am I sabotaging my professional future, my financial future by getting involved in a relationship with a man who doesn't have a clear plan for his life? You need to ask some of these questions;

- Does he have children?
- Is he current on his child support?
- Does he have a criminal record that will affect his ability to get a job?
- Does he have uncontrollable debt?
- Is he emotionally stable?
- Who reared him and did he have a stable growth environment?
- Will his emotional scars cause him to be abusive to me or my children?

- Will he share financial responsibility for taking care of household bills for me and my children?
- Will he support me in my professional goals?
- Can he tolerate me making more money than him?
- Does he want the same things in life that I want?
- Will he try to hinder me or sabotage my success just to keep me at his level?
- Will he come to my job and at a fool and try to get me fired if we don't work out?

Hannah refused to be hindered by Elkanah's limited expectations for her; Hannah knew that it was not enough just to be Elkanah's wife; she knew that she had to give birth to the purpose that God had placed inside of her. Hannah refused to surrender her destiny at the feet of her husband because Hannah understood that she, like us, owe God to become all who we are destined and designed by God to become. Hannah refused to become anybody's B.I.T.C.H.

6

GIVING BIRTH TO YOUR GREATER YOU

Each of us are in the process of becoming; with every second that passes we are no longer who we once were and we are in the constant state of becoming who we shall be; every moment that we live provide us with an opportunity to take in new information, to meet new people, to experience new happenings, and as a result we are always in a constant state of change, a perpetual state of becoming.

I watched a caterpillar crawl along the earth, navigating its way towards a tree, once at the tree the caterpillar proceeded to climb the tree and moved out onto the tree limb. The caterpillar began to weave its cocoon while hanging on a limb. Why out on a limb? Why not weave its cocoon attached to the secure footing of the base of tree?

The caterpillar knew something that I hadn't thought about; the caterpillar was not building its cocoon based upon its present condition, but the caterpillar was building its cocoon based upon its future expectation. The caterpillar knew that the chubby cumbersome body that it presently had was only temporary and through the process of metamorphism the caterpillar knew it was about to become something different, something better, something bolder, something more beautiful than what it currently was.

The caterpillar crawled towards its destiny, climbed towards its destiny, hung in there for its destiny, and broke through the cocoon for its destiny, and when the winds of opportunity blew; the butterfly which once was a caterpillar, flew into its destiny. I encourage you to not be ashamed of crawling until you are able to fly.

I have discovered that many people are embarrassed to admit that they are in a crawling stage of life, at a place of beginning, at a humble place where they are trying to get their footing and find their direction for destiny. The place of crawling is a place where God is allowing you to be purged of the vanity of arrogant pride in an effort to have you to understand that when you do begin to fly you are not to act arrogantly and pompous, but you are to maintain an attitude of gratitude and be willing to help someone else crawl their way into their destiny, as you serve as a mentor and role model who is flying high.

When the caterpillar is in the cocoon it knows that its time of being restrained by this tightly woven material in a dark, tough, and tight place is time limited, but it is a necessary process. When the caterpillar metamorphs into a butterfly and then begins the process of trying to break free, the butterfly is now discarding the very fabric it has woven to prepare itself for its destiny shift. The cocoon that the caterpillar needed to change into its new destiny image is now an encumbrance and hindrance to who the butterfly has now become. In order for the butterfly to 'be' all that it has now 'become', it must break through the very thing that it once needed to become what it is now.

If someone cuts open the cocoon to help the butterfly get out while it is struggling to escape the bondage of the cocoon, the butterfly will be crippled for life because it is in the butterfly's struggle to escape the cocoon that a special fluid is forced from the upper part of the butterfly's body into the wings of the butterfly. Once this fluid is forced into the wings of the butterfly, the butterfly now has the strength that its wings need to propel its self upon the winds of destiny; and the once fluid filled body has now been squeezed into flying shape. The struggles you are experiencing are strengthening your wings and squeezing you into flying shape.

The struggles and trials that we experience early on in life, especially those struggles we experience growing up, work together to shape and create our self image and psychological identity; the struggles of our growth environment is often the cocoon that we must often break through in order to fully 'become'. Our growth environment, where we were born, when we were born, and who we were born to, provides the 'crawling ground' in which we build our mental, physical, and spiritual endurance as we learn to maneuver around and over obstacles.

God has a plan for your life; the universe has a need for your existence! You are not an accident, a mistake, or a surprise. Your existence was preordained, well planned out, and carefully orchestrated; you have ***destinies*** to discover and purpose to fulfill. Yes I said destinies; and now let me tell you why I said it. As we are in the process of becoming, life will present us with what I call check points and at these check points we must have successfully learned from passed experiences, both good and bad. We must have obtained the wisdom we were suppose to learn from those past experiences in order to successfully navigate the checkpoint we are about to experience in the future.

Sometimes God allows an illness to become a checkpoint, the loss of a loved one, being downsized from a job, experiencing the pain of a failed relationship can be a checkpoint. A check point can be anything, a person or an event that causes your life to shake and become disrupted. You can pass through the next check point in life if you have successfully obtained the wisdom you were supposed to learn about yourself, others, and God when you passed through earlier checkpoints.

Have you ever wondered why some people always seem to be stuck in a desolate place in life? No matter how much they desire for their life to change for the better, they remain stuck. The reason why they remain in this undesired place is because they never face the facts about their present reality. They live in denial as to what part they continue to play in their own destruction, they blame the ex-wife, the ex-boyfriend, the mom who neglected them, the father who abandoned them, but they never come to the conclusion that says this; "I am not the only one to blame for my jacked up life, but I am 100 % responsible for where my life goes from here!"

It is up to you to determine what the next chapter of your life looks like; you are responsible for who you are becoming. You are responsible for giving birth to your God designed 'destiny you'! Yes there were some disappointing things that happened to you! Yes life has been unfair to you! Yes there are others who were born into a more privileged family than you, but every person has baggage that they must bear and no matter where you are born and who you are born to, baggage comes along with the trip called life.

Stop allowing your history to serve as a cell door that keeps you locked out of your future, instead learn to use your history, your unique story, as a ladder to elevate you to a higher height of understanding of who you presently are and who you are destined and designed by God to become. Now is your time to become your greater you!

7

A PRENATAL PRAISE

God was silent for 400 years, from the writing of the last chapter of the Old Testament Book of Malachi to the opening of the first New Testament Gospel, 400 years had past and God had not spoken through epiphany nor had God sent forth a prophet to proclaim God's message.

There are times in our life when it seems like God is giving us the silent treatment. We remember the promise of purpose and destiny that God spoke to our heart concerning our life, but then came the silence. How do you handle the silence? How do we deal with the seemingly absence of God's voice, care and concern for our struggle in pursuit of our God designed destiny? The experience of the silent treatment is a tormenting ordeal; sometimes children give their siblings or classmates the silent treatment as a way to show some type of displeasure with one's behavior. There are times when immature mates give each other the silent treatment as a form of punishment and signal of displeasure with the other. It is one thing to feel that a human being is giving you the silent treatment, but when it seems like God is giving you the silent treatment, that is certainly a higher level of emotional pain. If a man or woman is against me then I can take comfort in the fact that if God be for me then God is more than the world that is against me; but if it feels like God is against me then whole can I turn to plead my case?

God's silent treatment is not like the silent treatment that you and I may receive from human beings; whenever it seems like God is being silent, you can rest assured that God is working on your behalf behind the curtains of life. I have learned that even God's perceived silence speaks louder than the shouting of human beings. The Bible gives us insight regarding how God decided to break His silence over two thousand years ago when God sent the Angel Gabriel to deliver this message to the Virgin Mary,

Luke 1:26-35 (NKJV); 26 Now in the sixth month the
angel Gabriel was sent by God to a city of Galilee named
Nazareth, 27 to a virgin betrothed to a man whose name
was Joseph, of the house of David. The virgin's name
was Mary. 28 And having come in, the angel said to her,
"Rejoice, highly favored *one,* the Lord *is* with you; blessed
are you among women!" 29 But when she saw *him,* she
was troubled at his saying, and considered what manner
of greeting this was. 30 Then the angel said to her, "Do

not be afraid, Mary, for you have found favor with God. [31] And behold, you will conceive in your womb and bring forth a Son, and shall call His name JESUS (JEHOVAH IS SALVATION). [32] He will be great, and will be called the Son of the Highest; and the Lord God will give Him the throne of His father David. [33] And He will reign over the house of Jacob forever, and of His kingdom there will be no end." [34] Then Mary said to the angel, "How can this be, since I do not know a man?" [35] And the angel answered and said to her, "*The* **Holy Spirit** (hagios pneuma = sacred co-eternal and co-equal third person of the God-Head) will come upon you, and the power of the Highest will **overshadow you** (episkiazo =envelope /wrap you fully into His Self); therefore, also, that Holy One who is to be born will be called the Son of God.

After the Virgin Mary receives this message from God's angel, Mary is led by the Holy Spirit to visit her older cousin Elizabeth. The Bible says in **St. Luke 1:36-38 (NKJV);** [36] Now indeed, Elizabeth your relative has also conceived a son in her old age; and this is now the sixth month for her who was called barren. [37] For with God nothing will be impossible." [38] Then Mary said, "Behold the maidservant of the Lord! Let it be to me according to your word." And the angel departed from her.

God did not allow Mary, this young, poor and frighten teenager to go through the social, emotional, and biological hardship of being an unwed expecting mother alone. God directed Mary to go and see her older cousin Elizabeth who was already six months pregnant with the child who would become John the Baptist. God will provide us life coaches along the road of life. One of the biggest mistakes people make on the road of life is trying to do it all by themselves. Life is easier when you have life coaches, mentors, and spiritual elders whose wisdom can help you go farther and faster in life because you are wise and humble enough to gain insight from their life's journey.

Mary had to be terrified to be an unwed expecting mother during that day and time. She could have been stoned to death according to Old Testament Law if her husband to be, Joseph, had made any type of accusations against her regarding sexual immorality. The Virgin Mary was engaged to Joseph, the Old Testament word is betrothed, meaning she was pledged and devoted to Joseph and now God has interrupted her well planned life. Isn't that just like God, just when you seem to have your life planned the way you want it, God surprises you with a **'guess what'** moment?

Guess what Mary! You are about to become the Mother of God, you are about to carry ME, the Creator of Everything within the circumference of your virgin womb. Mary you are about to be recorded in history as the one and only Theotokos, the only one to carry God in her womb! Mary, I am placing myself into your womb so men and woman can one day receive me into their hearts.

God sent Mary to the house of her older cousin Elizabeth for several reasons, each of the reasons inspires Mary to understand that God will not allow Mary to go through this troublesome mystery of being the carrier of God's incarnation by her self. This very fact helps us to understand that having a seasoned, experienced, wise and faithful mentor to coach you 'through' and 'to' is important. Good coaches coach you through trails, troubles, and the pains of life; Good coaches not only coach you 'through', but they also coach you towards and 'to' your divine purpose, purposes, destiny and destines in life.

The Birthing Coach

Luke 1:36-37 (HCSB); [36]And consider your relative Elizabeth—even she has conceived a son in her old age, and this is the sixth month for her who was called childless. [37] For nothing will be impossible with God."

The Holy Spirit is our first birthing coach, because the Holy Spirit impregnates us with purpose. The Holy Spirit also directs us into the presence of the people God has called to help guide us towards our purposes and destinies. The Angel of God, Gabriel, told Mary that her older cousin was six months pregnant and Mary should go and visit her. Gabriel then says this in Luke 1, verse 37; For nothing will be impossible with God. This is the type of faith that God wants us to have, a faith that believes the impossible! A faith that chooses to believe God's Word above your circumstances!

Not only is Elizabeth older than Mary, she is also wiser, more mature and more experienced in life. Elizabeth had been trying to have a child for many years and now she is too old according to medical science. God waited for just the right time to allow Elizabeth to become pregnant by her husband Zechariah who was a temple priest. Look how God allowed Elizabeth to become pregnant after her natural time according to man's calendar and clock; yet God causes Mary to become pregnant as a young girl who is barely a teenager, Elizabeth becomes pregnant after her time and Mary becomes pregnant before her time. WOW!!! Mary was becoming pregnant too early according to man's clock and for Elizabeth it was too late for her to become pregnant according to man's clock. God's timing is always synchronized, perfected timing! God had both Mary and Elizabeth right where God needed for them to be; Mary and Elizabeth were walking in **synchronized faith**, living obedient lives in the perfect will of God; they were living by faith in the God Dimension where all things are possible and nothing is impossible.

As human beings we have our own sense of timing, we plan out our lives and develop 3 year plans, 5 year plans and even 10 year plans, this type of planning is good but always leave room for God to interrupt your plans with

His purpose. Be sure that your plans are driving you towards God's destinies and purposes for your life. Too many Elizabeth's in life get frustrated and feel defeated later on in life when they see the Mary's of the world about to give birth early in life. Stop comparing yourself to other people, when you compare yourself to other people success you come down with a case of the 'I Thought By Now' Syndrome. I thought by now I would have the house I want! I thought by now I would have the spouse I prayed for! I thought by now I would have the six figure job I have been striving for! God does not want us comparing ourselves to others, neither does God want us giving up on our hopes, dreams and aspirations because we are closer to Elizabeth's age and time than we are to Mary's age and time; God's timing is always perfect timing. **Galatians 6:9 (HCSB);** 9 So we must not get tired of doing good, for we will reap at the proper time if we don't give up.

Make My Baby Kick

Elizabeth coached Mary on how to become a soon to be mother and a soon to be wife. Wise people are willing to learn from others who have already successfully navigated the path that they are now about to travel. Good coaches provide constructive feedback and confirmation to those they are coaching and mentoring, In **Luke 1:39-45 (GW);** 39 Soon afterward, Mary hurried to a city in the mountain region of Judah.

40 She entered Zechariah's home and greeted Elizabeth.
41 When Elizabeth heard the greeting, she felt the baby
kick. Elizabeth was filled with the Holy Spirit.
42 She said in a loud voice, "You are the most blessed of
all women, and blessed is the child that you will have. 43 I
feel blessed that the mother of my Lord is visiting me.
44 As soon as I heard your greeting, I felt the baby jump
for joy. 45 You are blessed for believing that the Lord
would keep his promise to you."

A good birthing coach should have the power of God flowing in them to the degree that when you hear a Word, message, advice, direction from your coach, every now and then your 'DESTINY CHILD' should kick and leap in your spiritual womb! God allows your Destiny Child to kick every now and then just to confirm to you that your baby of purpose and destiny is still alive and kicking.

When God allows your water to break your destinies and purposes will be birthed. Elizabeth told Mary that the child I am carrying kicked, jumped and leaped when I heard your voice. This is why it is so important to guard your ears, guard your mind and guard your consciousness because just as faith comes by hearing the Word of God, doubt comes into your heart when your take in stuff that causes you to doubt God's promises for your life. Elizabeth tells Mary that Mary is blessed because Mary has believed that God will keep His promise to Mary. Faith is the primary ingredient needed to get God to move on your behalf.

Even the child that Elizabeth was carrying had enough spiritual intuition to give God a pre-natal praise for what was about to happen. The child that Elizabeth was carrying would be named John the Baptist and years later he would be the one who baptized Jesus, the child Mary was carrying.

Timing is everything in the God Dimension, the God dimension is that indescribable place beyond time and space where God's timing over rules human time. It is the space and place where water turns to wine, Red Seas part, and thousands are fed with two fish and five loaves of bread.

The God Dimension is where you are right now reading this book, you are becoming your greater you, in time, but no longer limited by a calendar or a watch. The enlightenment you are receiving right now has placed you in a different time zone where you now function according to God's divine timing.

The kicking of faith and leaping of hope you feel inside right now is your 'DESTINY CHILD' saying to you that your dreams are still alive. That pressure you feel in the mid-section of your body is your destinies and purposes trying to get out! The womb of your faith is becoming so full with the pressure of praise until you feel like your water is about to break sooner or later!

Mary knows that what she is being chosen by God to do

is not an easy task, but she chooses to give God a pre-natal praise in anticipation of the great thing that God is about to do in her life and in the history of the world. A pre-natal praise doesn't wait until God answers the prayer, a pre-natal praise thanks God in advance for what one's faith tells them that God is about to do. A pre-natal praise thanks God on credit, knowing by faith that God makes good on every promise that God makes.

Mary gives God a pre-natal praise in **Luke 1:46-56 (HCSB);** [46] And Mary said: My soul proclaims the greatness of the Lord, [47] and my spirit has rejoiced in God my Savior, [48] because He has looked with favor on the humble condition of His slave. Surely, from now on all generations will call me blessed, [49] because the Mighty One has done great things for me, and His name is holy. [50] His mercy is from generation to generation on those who fear Him. [51] He has done a mighty deed with His arm; He has scattered the proud because of the thoughts of their hearts; [52] He has toppled the mighty from their thrones and exalted the lowly. [53] He has satisfied the hungry with good things and sent the rich away empty. [54] He has helped His servant Israel, mindful of His mercy, [55] just as He spoke to our ancestors, to Abraham and his descendants forever. [56] And Mary stayed with her about three months; then she returned to her home.

8

WARS IN THE WOMB

As soon as God decided to allow you to be conceived in your mother's womb the devil had an assassinating assignment upon your life. Satan placed you on his demonic hit list, because Satan understands something about us as human beings that many fail to understand; the secret of your being and my being is this; you and I are born on purpose, born for purpose and born with purpose. Satan is determined to prevent you and I from achieving the God designed purpose and purposes that we were born to achieve.

It is a mistake to believe that Satan only begins to attack you once you are born, the truth of the matter is that just as in the last chapter I told you of the importance of having a pre-natal praise, Satan has what I call pre-natal attacks on our life. From the time your mother conceived you, you began to take in information, you began to become shaped, formatted, and developed based upon the biological, psychological, sociological and spiritual input that your mother took in. I learned in high school computer programming class that junk in equals junk out. If the computer is fed, programmed, and formatted with the wrong software then the information that the computer produces will be corrupted and useless. Children begin to learn even while still in the mother's womb.

According to psychology professor, Dr. Rick Gilmore of the Pennsylvania State University; "there is ample evidence that fetuses are picking up information from the outside world. They're especially receptive to sounds from the mother's body and the external environment. Gilmore also refers to a well-known study conducted by Anthony DeCasper at the University of South Carolina that seems to prove the existence of prenatal learning. Mothers were instructed to read Dr. Seuss out loud while they were pregnant, Gilmore explains. When the babies were born, researchers tested to see if they recognized Dr. Seuss against other stories, and their mother's voice against other readers. In both cases, the infants were able to pick up on the vocal patterns they'd become familiar with in utero. Gilmore states that hearing is one of the first senses to develop. As early as 16 weeks gestation, a developing fetus begins to perceive the world outside the womb through his or her fluid-filled ears. However, a sound-dampening barrier of embryonic fluid and abdominal tissue restricts audible input. The sound a fetus hears in the womb is highly muffled, consisting mostly of low frequencies, says Gilmore. Inside the womb, people's voices sound like

Charlie Brown's teacher, sort of like a muted trumpet. However there is a lot of information in that filtered and muted sound stream."

(http://news.psu.edu/story/141254/2009/02/23/research/probing-question-can-babies-learn-utero)

There is evidence that one of the earliest senses to develop in the fetus is the sense of hearing, this is not by accident, this is scientific evidence that faith comes through hearing, and faith is strengthened and developed by hearing God's Word. So if faith is built by hearing, then could it be that doubt, ignorance, racism, sexism, and foolishness is built by hearing the wrong thing?

It is distressing to see a pregnant mother cursing, listening to certain music that is negative and being engaged in conversations that are negative and destructive because her child is taking in all the garbage that the mother is listening to. This is the first of many pre-natal spiritual attacks that a child comes under while still in the mother's womb.

It is true for the most part that each of us are products of our environment, be it good or bad, but because of God's calling on our life, our future doesn't have to be limited because of the circumstances of our past. You have heard people talk about generational curses as if they are giving some credibility to witchcraft and voodoo, if you are a Christian believer who is covered by the blood of Jesus, no weapon formed against you will be able to prosper. Generational curses are not curses in the form of witchcraft, but we bring curses upon ourselves by repeating the same dysfunctional lifestyle and behaviors that our parents, grandparents, siblings and others in our family line did. This is the case in one of the Biblical stories we will examine in this chapter.

Here we encounter a family that looks happy on the outside, but it is sad behind closed doors. This should have been a time joy and celebration, but it is a time of tensions, turmoil, and despair. Esau has been deceived by his swindling brother Jacob out of his birthright, and now Jacob's and Esau's father Isaac has been deceived by Jacob and unwittingly given the family blessing to the second son Jacob instead of Esau the first born heir. To add to this dysfunctional family dynamic, Rebekah, who is Jacob's and Esau's mother, and Isaac's wife, was complicit in planning, plotting, aiding and abetting Jacob in deceiving the sons' father and her husband Isaac.

Genesis 25:19-22 (HCSB); [19] These are the family records of Isaac son of Abraham. Abraham fathered Isaac. [20] Isaac was 40 years old when he took as his wife Rebekah daughter of Bethuel the Aramean from Paddan-aram and sister of Laban the Aramean. [21] Isaac prayed to the LORD on behalf of his wife because she was childless. The LORD heard his prayer, and his wife Rebekah conceived. [22] But the children inside her struggled with each other, and she said, "Why is this happening to me?" So she went to inquire of the LORD.

Isaac, the son of Abraham and Sarah, prayed for his wife

Rebekah to be able to conceive and give birth to a child. Rebekah was having difficulty getting pregnant just like Sarah, Isaac's mother had difficulty getting pregnant. This represents the spiritual struggle to conceive a faith that is willing to wait on God's timing. God nurtures faith through the waiting process. A wise man once told me to be patient with God and to view my life like an airplane, he said; "small planes that only carry very small loads don't need a very large runway to take off from and they can get into the air pretty fast, but you Tobias LaGrone are not a small plane, you are a jumbo jet, God is equipping you to carry a heavy load of God's favor and divine responsibility, therefore the runway that God is building for your take off is taking longer than what you would like but it will be well worth the wait".

When Rebekah finally got pregnant she noticed that it felt like there was a war in her womb because her twin sons were fighting inside of her. Rebekah said that there was a struggle going on inside of her; I believe that there was both a physical struggle and spiritual struggle going on inside of Rebekah. Rebekah came from a pagan family, a family of idol worshippers, liars, scammers, thieves, and crooks. She struggled to let go of her old ways while learning to trust the God of Abraham, Sarah and Isaac.

The physical struggle in her womb was a physical manifestation of the psychological-spiritual battle that was happening in her mind and soul; "do I let go of the old and take hold of the new, or do I stick with old beliefs and behaviors that are comfortable but corrupted"?

Genesis 25:24-26 (HCSB); [24] When her time came to give birth, there were indeed twins in her womb. [25] The first one came out red-looking, covered with hair like a fur coat, and they named him Esau. [26] After this, his brother came out grasping Esau's heel with his hand. So he was named Jacob. Isaac was 60 years old when they were born.

Esau exited his mother's womb first, and Jacob, his twin brother, was literally right on Esau's heels. Jacob had his hand firmly wrapped around Esau's heel as to say that you don't deserve to be the first born, I should be the first born. The war in Rebekah's womb was a struggle for position, power, and possessions. Instead of the two brothers fighting and becoming weaker through division, they could have been working together and becoming stronger through unity.

God would have rather had Jacob's hand wrapped around Esau's ankle as a way of Jacob to PUSH his brother Esau towards his destiny. God would have rather had Jacob's hand wrapped around Esau's ankle as a way for Esau to PULL his brother Jacob towards his destiny. You need people in your life that will PUSH you to become your greater you! You also need people in your life that will PULL you up to a higher level of living, being and becoming. Jacob's and Esau's relationship was contaminated and sabotaged by their parents' unresolved family dynamics and psychological-spiritual issues.

Genesis 25:27-28 (HCSB); [27]When the boys grew up, Esau became an expert hunter, an outdoorsman, but Jacob was a quiet man who stayed at home. [28] Isaac loved Esau because he had a taste for wild game, but Rebekah loved Jacob.

The war in Rebekah's womb continued outside of her womb as evidenced by Jacob's and Esau's continued struggles with each other. To make matters worse, Isaac and Rebekah allowed their own unresolved childhood issues to effect how they would rear Esau and Jacob; the scripture says that Isaac loved/favored Esau and Rebekah loved/favored Jacob. How does it feel to be a child who knows that your parent(s) favors one of your siblings over you? This happens everyday in our world, and the sad reality is that no one discusses it.

It is important that every parent and child understands the natural human tendency for a parent to 'favor' one child over another, but this fact should not diminish the level of love that the parent gives to each child. One of the keys to successfully nurturing healthy emotional development in your children is learning to love each of them equally, while simultaneously loving them differently according to each child's unique personality traits and emotional needs. Loving your children differently does not mean you have to love them unequally.

It is possible that the struggle between Esau and Jacob is dysfunctional generational residue from both Rebekah's and Isaac's family bloodline; there is not much Biblical information regarding details of Rebekah's early growth years, but there is plenty of information about Isaac's early developmental growth environment. See Isaac was suppose to be Abraham's and Sarah's firstborn child but Abraham had a son by Sarah's slave girl Hagar before Sarah conceived Isaac.

Before there was a war in the womb between Esau and Jacob, there was a different type of womb war between Ishmael and Isaac. This womb war took place within the incubating womb of Abraham's and Sarah's house. Once again, the struggle of the children was caused by the unresolved dysfunctional issues and choices of the parents. Let us examine the choices of Abraham and Sarah, Isaac's parents and Jacob and Esau's grandparents, and let us see how the present day issues between Jacob and Esau are connected to the poor past choices of their grandparents.

While growing up I would often hear family members say; "what goes around, comes around and what goes up must come down". This was their way of saying that everybody gets back from life what they put out in life. As a pastoral psycho-therapist I often have clients who can't figure out why they have certain dysfunctional behavioral traits and self-sabotaging habits, what we often discover is that these behaviors are subconscious learned behaviors that were picked up from one's growth environment as a child or teen and this is what has been keeping the person from reaching their full personal and professional potential. Once we discover the source of the issues we are able to address the issue and correct the issue.

Generational curses don't come from witches or warlocks, generational curses come from us repeating the same dysfunctional behaviors, and making the same poor choices that our parents and grandparents made.

In spiritual warfare analysis I have discovered this fact; "the generational demons that my parents and grandparents did not conquer are the same demons that will attack me and those family members in my generation". When grandparents and parents fail to tell the next generation about their personal struggles, spiritual struggles and the deep dark struggles that have plagued them, then they selfishly allow the next generation to go out into the world as sheep among demonic wolves.

If I had known what demons to be on the look out for then maybe I could have avoided some of the pits I fell into. You and I owe it to our children and the next generation to tell them the truth about the generational demons of alcoholism, drug addiction, adultery, pornography, stealing, lying, cheating, hustling, molestation, pedophilia, anger, domestic violence, etc., that has plagued us and others in our family line.

See Me, Love Me and Don't Misuse Me

Isaac's sons, Jacob and Esau, unknowingly ended up playing out the same type of spiritual struggle that took place between Isaac and Ishmael, a struggle that was placed into motion by the actions of Abraham (Abram) and Sarah (Sarai). **Genesis 16:1-3 (HCSB)** 1 Abram's wife Sarai had not borne any children for him, but she owned an Egyptian slave named Hagar. 2 Sarai said to Abram, "Since the LORD has prevented me from bearing children, go to my slave; perhaps through her I can build a family." And Abram agreed to what Sarai said. 3 So Abram's wife Sarai took Hagar, her Egyptian slave, and gave her to her husband Abram as a wife for him. This happened after Abram had lived in the land of Canaan for 10 years.

Hagar is given by Sarai to Abram in order for Hagar to give a child to Abram and Sarai, there is no conversation regarding what Hagar wants. There is no dialogue in regard to how Hagar feels about Sarai's idea. Hagar was given as property to Abraham; Hagar was not given the opportunity to experience the joys of dating, she was denied the romantic experiences of courtship and being wooed by a beloved. She was denied the joy of receiving roses just because. She was denied the experience of deciding; do I say 'I do', Hagar was told to say yes to

Sarai's demand or else she would be punished.

Sarai doesn't 'SEE' Hagar as being a woman with worth, she only sees Hagar as an object she can use to attempt to circumvent God's choice of withholding a child from Sarai. In an African Village the people of that village greet each other with the greeting of Sawubona. It's an African Zulu greeting that means "I see you." It has a long oral history, and it means more that our traditional "hello." It means, I see your personality. I see your humanity. I see your dignity and human worth. I see you as a person, I see you as a human being who has value, worth and dignity.

You must learn to see and value your own God designed worth, because if you don't nobody else will. Hagar may have been Sarai's slave girl, but Hagar knew that she was more than a slave girl in the eyes of God. Hagar knew that God saw her even when others looked past her, looked over her, looked through her and when Sarai looked down on her.

Abraham was 75 years old, and Sarah was 65 year olds when God promised to give them a son, but after 24 years of waiting on God both Abraham and Sari became inpatient waiting on God to keep His promise to them. Sarai decided to help God out by making her slave girl Hagar become Abraham's second wife. I have learned over the years that God doesn't need my help to fulfill the promises and plans He has for my life; what God needs from me and you is our cooperation and obedience. When we take matters into our own hands we are not only working against God, we are also working against our own best interest because God's plans are based on our long term destiny and not our short term satisfaction.

Hagar acquiesces to Abraham's and Sarah's request, and she agrees to marry Abraham. When Hagar becomes pregnant Sarah becomes angry and jealous towards Hagar and begins to treat her very badly; **Genesis 16:4-6
(HCSB);** 4 He slept with Hagar, and she became
pregnant. When she (Hagar) realized that she was
pregnant, she treated her mistress (Sarah) with contempt.
5 Then Sarai said to Abram, "You are responsible for my
suffering! I put my slave in your arms, and ever since she
saw that she was pregnant, she has treated me with
contempt. May the LORD judge between me and you."
6 Abram replied to Sarai, "Here, your slave is in your
hands; do whatever you want with her." Then Sarai
mistreated her so much that she ran away from her.

Sarah is disappointed with how things are turning out, but she should not be surprised that her little scheme didn't work out just like she planned it. Sarah is angry with Abraham for following Sarah's own advice and taking Hagar to be his wife. Sarah is angry with Hagar because Sarah believes since Hagar has been married to Abraham, she has not been an obedient slave girl. Well, I would dare to say that when the slave girl marries the owner of the house she will no longer consider herself a slave girl, but she now sees herself as an equal partner in the family dynamic. Don't allow people to keep you small when God is elevating you! Hagar understood that she is no longer Hagar's slave girl; she is now Abraham's wife.

I imagine Hagar was saying to herself;

"Let me get this straight in my mind. Sarah, you tell your husband that you want him to marry me, have sex with me, make love to me, and get me pregnant in order for you to have a son. Sarah, you know that I am your slave girl and I have to obey you and marry Abraham, I marry Abraham and become pregnant and now you are angry and jealous, because I have enough sense to stop acting like your servant and start acting like his wife? Secondly Sarah: you are giving me to your husband and you are asking me to allow him to make love to me with out him ***'feeling love'*** for me. Sarah you are asking me to allow him to make love to me without me ***'feeling love'*** for him. You must think that I am a mechanical toy, an android, a robot. You must really think that I am like a child's doll that has hands that can't feel, eyes that can't see and a heart that can't feel. Sarah you are asking me to commit to the sacrifice of love without enjoying the benefits of loving and being loved. Sarah, I need you to understand that I am not a 'thing' to be used; I am a woman who loves and needs to be loved. You ask me to give your husband Abraham my all, I gave him my all and now I will enjoy the benefits of all he is and all he has. I am no longer your slave; I am Abraham's wife!"

Now Sarah is angry because Hagar eyes have become open, her conscience has become enlightened! Hagar now understands that her ***elevation*** to being Abraham's wife ***changed her position*** of being Sarah's slave. Your mind is the first battlefield Satan will attack you on; you can only rise as high as you can think. You will have what you believe in alignment with God's destiny will for your life, but first you have to believe it (seeing it through the lens of faith), before you see it happen/manifest in the physical realm.

This is what salvation through Jesus Christ does for us; salvation in Jesus Christ elevates us from the bondage of Satan and sin and elevates us into a royal place of authority and power in God's kingdom plan. Salvation through Jesus Christ crumbles all the walls that divide us and seek to classify one person as being more valuable than the other. Jesus Christ knocked down the walls of classism, racism, sexism and economic superiority based upon income and zip codes; **Galatians 3:27-29 (NKJV);**
[27] For as many of you as were baptized into Christ have
put on Christ. [28] There is neither Jew nor Greek, there is
neither slave nor free, there is neither male nor female;
for you are all one in Christ Jesus. [29] And if you *are*
Christ's, then you are Abraham's seed, and heirs
according to the promise.

Hagar I See You

Genesis 16:4-6 (HCSB); [4] He slept with Hagar, and she became pregnant. When she realized that she was pregnant, she treated her mistress with contempt. [5] Then Sarai said to Abram, "You are responsible for my suffering! I put my slave in your arms, and ever since she saw that she was pregnant, she has treated me with contempt. May the LORD judge between me and you."
[6] Abram replied to Sarai, "Here, your slave is in your hands; do whatever you want with her." Then Sarai mistreated her so much that she ran away from her.

Abraham was supposed to protect Hagar from the mistreatment of Sarah, but instead of speaking up to protect the woman carrying his child, he abandoned Hagar and left her defenseless against the verbal and physical abuse that Sarah inflicted upon her. What Abraham and Sarah didn't realize is that Hagar was a test sent by God, God knew that Sarah would take matters into her own hands and give Hagar to Abraham as a wife in order to make sure that the promise of Abraham having a son was fulfilled.

Abraham and Sarah didn't understand that God was delaying the promise to give Sarah a child, because Abraham and Sarah had not matured enough in their faith, character, patience and compassion for others. This was evident in the way Abraham and Sarah were mistreating Hagar! At this point on their spiritual odyssey Abraham and Sarah names have not been changed, they are still called by their pre-transformational names of Abram and Sarai.

They were waiting on God to move on their behalf, yet God was waiting on them to grow up and become whom God knew God created them to be from the inside out. Sarah was complaining that she could not become pregnant with a child, but God wanted her to first become pregnant with faith. You need ***pregnant faith*** in order to give birth to your God-designed destiny!

Abraham's negligence and Sarah's abuse towards Hagar would reverberate through the family blood line. The child that Hagar was carrying experienced the same pain and abuse that his mother experienced. Not only would it come back to haunt Abraham and Sarah, it would also haunt their yet to be born son Isaac, and their future grandsons, Jacob and Esau.

Hagar got tired of being mistreated by Sarah and she did what most of us do when we are in a place that we feel we are no longer welcomed, Hagar ran away! **Genesis 16:7-8 (HCSB);** 7 The Angel of the LORD found her by a spring of water in the wilderness, the spring on the way to Shur. 8 He said, "Hagar, slave of Sarai, where have you come from and where are you going?" She replied, "I'm running away from my mistress Sarai."

After Hagar runs away, we encounter Hagar at a water spring that is on the road to a place called Shur, this is a place southwest of Palestine on the eastern border or within the border of Egypt; the Israelites passed through the wilderness of Shur after crossing the Red Sea. Hagar's ethnicity was Egyptian and therefore it was not by accident that she chose a road that would lead her back home to Egypt, but before she could make it home to her family, friends, and kindred, God sends an angel to help Hagar pause and process what she is about to do. No, God did not condone Hagar being mistreated by Sarah, but God wanted Hagar to understand that some good could come from her pain.

It is not by accident or happen-chance that God directs His angel to ask Hagar these specific questions; where have you come from and where are you going? God wants Hagar to psychologically process what she is doing and why she is doing it. Could God be saying; "Hagar stop and think about what you are doing, you are running back home to Egypt, and you know what you left in Egypt; yes the thoughts of home are comforting when you are in a place of trouble, trial, and struggle, but make sure that you are consciously aware and understand that when you run from one thing you are running into something else that may be better, or it could end up being worse. Hagar you know what you left in Egypt, so why don't you trust me to guide you forward to a brighter future. You can't grow forward walking backwards! Going back to Egypt is not the answer, but going back to the place where I have planted you in this season of your life is stepping forward into your destiny."

Genesis 16:8-10 (HCSB); [9] Then the Angel of the LORD said to her, "You must go back to your mistress and submit to her mistreatment." When I was young in the Christian faith, I had extreme difficulty with the instructions that the angel gave to Hagar, why would you make a woman who is being abused, return to an abusive situation. As I have matured in the Christian faith, I have discovered that my focus was placed on the wrong word, I spent too much time being upset about the word 'mistreatment' and placed too little emphasis in the word 'submit'. The Hebrew word for submit is *anah* which literally means to humble yourself. Make yourself mentally palatable and teachable. Instead of looking upon Sarah's mistreatment of you as a curse, look at it as preparation for your own elevation! I discovered that the Hebrew meaning of Hagar's name means flight or the one who runs; why is this important, because God wants us to see that you can't achieve destiny and become your greater you by running from your struggles. No, God is not telling you to stay in a domestic violence situation, be it at home or on a job where you are terribly mistreated, what God is saying is don't leave without a plan. God is saying don't leave empty handed!

The Hebrew word for mistreatment is *tachath* which means to put yourself under one's authority for the sake of **getting something in return for the hell they are putting you through**. There is an exchange in, and a return for, you are trading in your pain in exchange for the treasure of purpose and destiny!

Hagar, God is directing you to exchange your services as a maid in return for Sarai teaching you how to be a Princess. Sarah's name was Sarai before God later changed it; Sarai means Princess in the Hebrew language. Hagar, Sarai doesn't realize that as you watch her operate in her royalty, she is teaching you how to be royal. Sarai doesn't realize that while she is directing her kingdom, she is teaching you how to rule the kingdom that will be birthed out of you. Hagar there is a **promise** attached to your **pain**! This is important because of this verse;
Genesis 16:10-11 (HCSB); [10] The Angel of the LORD also said to Hagar, "I will greatly multiply your offspring,
and they will be too many to count." [11] Then the Angel
of the LORD said to her: You have conceived and will have a son. You will name him Ishmael for the Lord has heard your cry of affliction.

Hagar will give birth to a son and God has directed her to name him Ishmael, which means, God will hear, or God has heard my cry of affliction. Hagar gave birth to Ishmael, and he became a King of the Arabian Nation, the father of Islam and the father of 12 Arabian Princes
as recorded in **Genesis 25:12-16 (HCSB);** [12] These are
the family records of Abraham's son Ishmael, whom Hagar the Egyptian, Sarah's slave, bore to Abraham.
[13] These are the names of Ishmael's sons; their names according to the family records are: Nebaioth, Ishmael's

firstborn, then Kedar, Adbeel, Mibsam, [14] Mishma, Dumah, Massa, [15] Hadad, Tema, Jetur, Naphish, and Kedemah. [16] These are Ishmael's sons, and these are their names by their villages and encampments: 12 leaders (Princes) of their clans.

We know that the Messianic promise of Jesus Christ comes through Isaac, Abraham's second son and the first born of Abraham with Sarah, but God has blessed the seed of Ishmael forever and man can not curse what God has blessed. To go to war with Islam is to go to war with God Himself. God had a purpose and has a purpose for the seed of Ishmael and the Arabian Nation that is beyond our finite scope and what we should do is trust God to be God.

Genesis 16:13-14 (HCSB); [13] So she called the LORD who spoke to her: The God Who Sees (El Ro'iy), for she said, "In this place, have I actually seen the One who sees **me**?" Hagar is declaring that she has gained a psychological spiritual consciousness of understanding that she is important to God. Even though she is considered by Sarai as only a slave girl, God informs Hagar that she is born on purpose, born for purpose and born with purpose. **Genesis 16:14 (HCSB);** [14] That is why she named the spring, "**A Well of the Living One Who Sees Me**." It is located between Kadesh and Bered. (Hagar named the God who she met El Ro'iy and she named the place where she met God Beer-lahai-roi, meaning the well of the Living One seeing me. Hagar is testifying to us today that God will always provide a place for His children to meet Him and drink of His Living Water. While you are waiting for your water to break, your destiny to be fulfilled, and your purpose to be released in the earth, God wants us to drink of the cool refreshing water of the Holy Spirit. The Holy Spirit will comfort and guide us on the road of life.

You may feel that you are alone and that nobody cares about the struggles you are going through, but I want you to know that God sees you and God hears your cry. The Bible declares in **Psalm 34:15-19 (NKJV);** 15 The eyes of the LORD *are* on the righteous, And His ears *are open* to their cry. 16 The face of the LORD *is* against those who do evil, to cut off the remembrance of them from the earth. 17 *The righteous* cry out, and the LORD hears, And delivers them out of all their troubles. 18 The LORD *is* near to those who have a broken heart, And saves such as have a contrite spirit. 19 Many *are* the afflictions of the righteous, But the LORD delivers him out of them all.

9

SURVIVING THE PREGNANT PAUSE

The dreams that Joseph had when he was 17 years old were in fact covenant promises that God was making to Joseph concerning God's destiny will for Joseph's life. Joseph was given the dream at the age of 17 years old but Joseph would be 30 years old when he walked into his destiny as Prime Minister of Egypt. Joseph, the Hebrew son of Jacob would become the Prime Minister of Egypt. Joseph would have to wait 13 years before his God designed destiny came to pass. Joseph would have to live in what I describe as a 'pregnant pause' for 13 years before he could give birth to his God designed destiny. We read the story and we know upfront that it would take 13 years for all of this to happen, but Joseph had no idea how long it would be before God's plan for his life culminated in his dreams coming to fruition.

One of the greatest struggles I have had on the road to becoming my 'destiny me', has been the struggle of waiting; exercising patience is not as easy as it sounds. I have struggled most of my life with learning how to be patient, especially when you I am waiting in an uncomfortable place. It is frustrating to know God has the power to change my circumstances for the better with a snap of His finger, but God chooses to make me wait; God insists that I experience the waiting period and maturing season of the pregnant pause.

God allows us to go through pregnant pauses because there is a whole lot that we need to learn between the time we receive the promise and the time we walk into our destiny. While you are waiting for God to break you through to your next dimension of purpose and destiny, 'learn not to waste your wait'. Don't waste your wait! Waiting is a form of worship to God that should not be wasted, the period of the pregnant pause is not a time for you to set idly by just waiting; NO, this is a time for you to be sharpening your skills, developing your character and nourishing the spiritual twins of purpose and destiny you are carrying within you.

Let's examine how God developed the person Joseph, for the position of destiny, during Joseph's pregnant pause. This is important because a position doesn't make you a better person, the position you hold is only as valuable, honored and dignified as the person who holds the position. Our world is wounded, broken, and corrupt because so many people thought that a new title or professional position would finally give them a sense of validation. The pregnant pause is more about **you**

becoming your **'better you'** while you are on the road to destiny.

God is changing the conditions in your place of promise while he is developing the character, dignity, and humility inside of you. If you were to walk into your place of destiny and purpose today, you would not be ready for the place and the place would not be ready for you. Transformation happens over a period of time; don't become frustrated with the wait!

Joseph's Journey with Time

Even though most of us know that God is up to something good in our life, waiting is still difficult. It has been said that good things come to those who wait, this may be true, but what they failed to tell me is how long I would have to wait for those good things to come. Dr. David Emery Mercer, in his book, Kierkegaard's Living Room, educates us on the relation between faith and history in philosophical fragments, whereas God's plan is active in history working on behalf of God's purpose, yet the most important history of them all is your history, your time and how you identify the hand of God working in your life.

My analysis of Kierkegaard informs me that there is an Outer history and an Inner History; an analysis of your Inner History causes you to engage in intrapersonal psychological-spiritual inventory, whereas you look back over your life and think of those significant events and important choices which have led you to your present 'now'. Your 'now' and my 'now' is a result of a choice, decision, and event that happened in the time frame of 'back then'. 'Back then' describes the past, now describes the present, and 'later on' describes the future that is yet to come. Your struggle to become the 'who' God created you to be is connected to the time in which you were birthed. The **'who'** is connected to the **'when'**; the 'who' of who you have become and are becoming is intrinsically interconnected to the **when** in **time** you were born.

Harriet Tubman, Fredrick Douglas, Winston Churchill, Martin Luther, Oprah Winfrey, Martin Luther King, Jr., Bill Gates, Steve Jobs, Warren Buffet and Barack Obama are just a few examples of the person being in place at the right God designed time. God designed the person, personality, persona, to fit the time in which one was born; if you take any of the people I mentioned and place them in a different time and place in history, we may have never known their names. God is using the pregnant pauses in your life to get you ready for 'your time' and to get the place of your time ready for you!

You were not born just to come into the world and occupy space and wander through time aimlessly, each of us were born for specific purposes in order to achieve specific God designed destinies. **Galatians 4:4-7 (ESV):**
4 But when the fullness of time had come, God sent

forth his Son, born of woman, born under the law, [5] to redeem those who were under the law, so that we might receive adoption as sons.[6] And because you are sons, God has sent the Spirit of his Son into our hearts, crying, "Abba! Father!" [7] So you are no longer a slave, but a son/daughter, and if a son/daughter, then an heir through God.

The Greek word for fullness is pleroma, meaning a full ship that is completely packed and filled with goods and crew. The birth of Jesus Christ was God sending Himself in the shipping vessel of flesh named Jesus, Jesus would become the Christ by being obedient unto death. The birth of Jesus Christ causes chronos, man's time to encounter, kairos, God's perfect timing. Success or failure in life depends on your ability to walk in **synchronized faith** with God's timing. **Galatians 6:9-10 (ESV):** [9] And let us not grow weary of doing good, for in **due season** we will reap, if we do not give up. [10] So then, as we have opportunity, let us do good to everyone, and especially to those who are of the household of faith.

Due season is the time of Kairos; the time of a fixed and definite time, the time when things are brought to a head, a time when the volcano of purpose has to explode. Kairos is God's unstoppable will colliding with man's agenda, and man's self-will agenda crumbles under the pressure of God's divine plan and kingdom destiny for your life. Due season is when you have to give birth because the womb of destiny can no longer contain the destiny child that you are carrying.

Joseph was the youngest son of Israel, Jacob's name had been changed to Israel, remember how Jacob swindled his brother Esau out of his birthright, well Jacob is an old man now, but he has a new heart. No longer is he called Jacob, but God has changed his name to Israel. Israel is the person of destiny that God designed and destined the man Jacob to become; now in his old age, living in his authentic self, Jacob/Israel feels that all is well in his life. The Bible says in Genesis 37:3-4 (ESV);
[3] Now Israel loved Joseph more than any other of his sons, because he was the son of his old age. And he made him a robe of many colors. [4] But when his brothers saw that their father loved him more than all his brothers, they hated him and could not speak peacefully to him.

Joseph's brothers hated him because he was favored by his father, everybody will not be happy about the favor that God the Father has placed upon you. The coat of many colors, the rainbow coat, was an outward visible sign of the favor that Joseph's father had placed upon Joseph's life.

I would like to present to you the idea that one of the reasons Israel favored and loved Joseph so much is because when Israel looked at Joseph, he was actually looking at the type of young man he wished he could have been. I imagine that Israel regrets his 'Jacob days', those days when Jacob would do anything to have his way and get what he wanted. Israel looks at his favored son Joseph and he believes that Joseph will not have to go through all the hell he went through in order to become who God designed and destined him to become.

Genesis 37:5-8 (NLT); [5]One night Joseph had a dream, and when he told his brothers about it, they hated him more than ever. [6] "Listen to this dream," he said. [7]"We were out in the field, tying up bundles of grain. Suddenly my bundle stood up, and your bundles all gathered around and bowed low before mine!" [8] His brothers responded, "So you think you will be our king, do you? Do you actually think you will reign over us?" And they hated him all the more because of his dreams and the way he talked about them.

When Joseph dreamed, God was allowing him to look into his own God-designed future through the eyes of God. Joseph saw symbols which represented his brothers bowing down in his presence. When Joseph told his brothers about the dream God had placed in his psyche, his brothers became even more envious towards Joseph. You can not tell everybody about what God has placed within your mind and heart; even some of your own family members will not be happy about where God is taking you in life.

Some people can only handle you when you are on the same level that they are, but when God begins to elevate you above them, then they don't know how to rejoice over your success. Stop flying low with people who don't want to see you fly high! Beware of people who can only relate to you when you are struggling, because people like this will work hard to make you feel comfortable in your misery; misery loves company! If you don't change your thinking, more years will pass, and you will still be stuck in a place of mental, physical and spiritual misery.

Genesis 37:9-11 (NLT); [9] Soon Joseph had another dream, and again he told his brothers about it. "Listen, I have had another dream," he said. "The sun, moon, and eleven stars bowed low before me!" [10] This time he told the dream to his father as well as to his brothers, but his father scolded him. "What kind of dream is that?" he asked. "Will your mother and I and your brothers actually come and bow to the ground before you?" [11] But while his brothers were jealous of Joseph, his father wondered what the dreams meant.

Whereas Joseph's first dream dealt with Joseph's family in the land of Canaan, the second dream was a destiny glimpse into Joseph's future impact in the land of Egypt. Joseph's father was astonished at the dream that Joseph told him. Israel, like any loving parent, wanted his son Joseph spared from the process and pain of becoming, but God had other plans for Joseph and the pain of the process would be unavoidable for Joseph. Joseph's journey with time began with his dreams.

Genesis 37:12-20 (NLT); [12] Soon after this, Joseph's brothers went to pasture their father's flocks at

Shechem. [13] When they had been gone for some time, Jacob said to Joseph, "Your brothers are pasturing the sheep at Shechem. Get ready, and I will send you to them." "I'm ready to go," Joseph replied. [14] "Go and see how your brothers and the flocks are getting along," Jacob said. "Then come back and bring me a report." So Jacob sent him on his way, and Joseph traveled to Shechem from their home in the valley of Hebron. [15] When he arrived there, a man from the area noticed him wandering around the countryside. "What are you looking for?" he asked. [16] "I'm looking for my brothers," Joseph replied. "Do you know where they are pasturing their sheep?" [17] "Yes," the man told him. "They have moved on from here, but I heard them say, 'Let's go on to Dothan.'" So Joseph followed his brothers to Dothan and found them there. [18] When Joseph's brothers saw him coming, they recognized him in the distance. As he approached, they made plans to kill him. [19] "Here comes the dreamer!" they said. [20] "Come on, let's kill him and throw him into one of these cisterns. We can tell our father, 'A wild animal has eaten him.' Then we'll see what becomes of his dreams!"

When Joseph's brothers saw him coming, they allowed Satan to convince them that the dreams and dreamer had to die. They were angry at the anointing that God had placed on Joseph's life, and they envied the favor that Israel had given to Joseph. Their goal was to erase Joseph, erase the dreams, erase the dreamer, erase the memory of the one they saw being favored by the father and elevated by God.

When you began to break free from the dysfunctional relationships in your life and begin to take control of your future and destiny, Satan and his demons will come at you even harder. Domestic violence is not only about the horrific violence, but it is about the perpetrator feeling that he/she has the right, power and authority to shape and control your very being. They want to become your god! When you resist their controlling ways, they attempt to erase you through verbal abuse by diminishing your self worth; or they will eventually try to murder you in order to permanently erase you. Satan despises those he can not control.

When you begin to break away from this controlling spirit of witchcraft and manipulation then the perpetrator becomes even more influenced by Satan to try and erase you from time. That is what murder is about, the demonic influence in the psyche and soul of a person to feel that they have the right to erase another life from the dimension of time. Joseph's brothers could not control him, so they decided to erase him!

Genesis 37:21-25 (NLT); [21] But when Reuben heard of
their scheme, he came to Joseph's rescue. "Let's not kill
him," he said. [22] "Why should we shed any blood? Let's
just throw him into this empty cistern here in the
wilderness. Then he'll die without our laying a hand on
him." Reuben was secretly planning to rescue Joseph and
return him to his father. [23] So when Joseph arrived, his

brothers ripped off the beautiful robe he was wearing.
24 Then they grabbed him and threw him into the cistern.
Now the cistern was empty; there was no water in it.
25 Then, just as they were sitting down to eat, they
looked up and saw a caravan of camels in the distance
coming toward them. It was a group of Ishmaelite
traders taking a load of gum, balm, and aromatic resin
from Gilead down to Egypt.

Not only did his brothers attack him, but they tore and ripped the beautiful robe that Joseph's father had given him. In the spiritual realm the act of tearing and ripping Joseph's robe is equivocal to how Satan uses people to tear and rip at your self esteem and personal identity. They try to convince you that you are not a person of worth and value, and as a result you should spend your time and energy trying to win their approval, this is a trick of the devil.

They thought they were erasing Joseph's destiny by destroying Joseph's coat of many colors, but what they failed to realize is that Joseph's outer coat was only a reflection of Joseph's inner God-designed destiny. They could take his coat, his outer identity, but they could not destroy his God designed identity and purpose. Knowing who you are in Jesus Christ will give you the power to overcome the spirits of low self esteem, low self worth and low self value. When you begin to value yourself, others will begin to value you as well. Your inner being will believe what ever your mind and spirit tells it to believe. You will have better when you begin to believe for better! You will have greater when you begin to believe that you deserve greater!

Joseph's brothers sold Joseph to slave traders who were on their way to Egypt to sell slaves. At this juncture Joseph's brothers feel they have erased Joseph from their life, they feel they have nullified Joseph's dreams by hurting the dreamer. Little did they realize that God was moving the pieces on the chess board of Joseph's life as God allowed Joseph's brothers dysfunctional behavior to be used as boat paddles to help row Joseph closer to his God designed destiny.

Destiny is not always pretty, destiny steps and destiny places can be ugly, cold, deep, dark and damp like the empty well that Joseph was thrown into. When you find yourself in similar troublesome situations on your way towards your destiny, please remember that God is using the struggle to strengthen you and grow you. The prize of destiny is not found in the destination itself, but is in the 'greater you' that you become during the process of destiny growth.

Joseph did not realize that God did not intend for the 17 year old Joseph to be the one to walk into the place of purpose and destiny; Joseph was not yet wise enough, experienced enough, mature enough, seasoned enough, nor was he rooted in the God of Abraham, Isaac, and Jacob (Israel) enough to walk directly into his place of purpose at the age of 17 years of age. God was going to use the next 13 years of Joseph's life to take him on a spiritual odyssey of self discovery and spiritual growth.

Joseph received the promise of greatness at the age of 17 but Joseph would be 30 years old before the promise came to pass. Wait on God; "**Habakkuk 2:3 (HCSB);** [3] For the vision is yet for **<u>the appointed time</u>**; it testifies about the end and will not lie. Though it delays, **<u>wait for it</u>**, since it will certainly come and not be late."

God has appointed the times, places and dates for every one of your breakthroughs to take place; your job is to live out each day by faith, and move forward through life and meet God at the appointed destinations in time. When you show up at your faith destinations, God will already have prepared a table before you in the presence of your enemies.

Haters Can't Stop God's Favor

Genesis 39:1 (NLT); [1] When Joseph was taken to Egypt by the Ishmaelite traders, he was purchased by Potiphar, an Egyptian officer. Potiphar was captain of the guard for Pharaoh, the king of Egypt.

Look how God's favor continues to follow Joseph; he was favored by his father Israel and when Joseph was sold into slavery, out of all the places and people Joseph could have been sold to, God orchestrated for Joseph to be sold to the captain of Pharoah's royal guard, Potiphar.

God also favored Joseph's professional development; **Genesis 39:2-4 (NLT);** [2] The LORD was with Joseph, so he succeeded in everything he did as he served in the home of his Egyptian master. [3] Potiphar noticed this and realized that the LORD was with Joseph, giving him success in everything he did. [4] This pleased Potiphar, so he soon made Joseph his personal attendant. He put him in charge of his entire household and everything he owned.

Potiphar orientated Joseph as to how he expected his estate to be run; Joseph was so successful in running the business affairs of Potiphar's estate that Potiphar promoted Joseph to the executive position of Potiphar's personal assistant. Joseph was sold into slavery by his brothers, **sold as a slave** to Potiphar by the slave traders, and now Joseph is being elevated from a slave position to an **executive position**.

Lesson of Humility

Genesis 39:5-6 (NLT); [5] From the day Joseph was put in charge of his master's household and property, the LORD began to bless Potiphar's household for Joseph's sake. All his household affairs ran smoothly, and his crops and livestock flourished. [6] So Potiphar gave Joseph complete administrative responsibility over everything he owned. With Joseph there, he didn't worry about a thing—except what kind of food to eat! Joseph was a very handsome and well-built young man.

Even though Potiphar did not know Joseph's God, the God of Abraham, Isaac, and Jacob (Israel), God blessed Potiphar for being obedient as he listened to God's directive whispers to purchase Joseph and promote Joseph. One of the truest signs of God's favor and anointing on your life is that you can bless others while you are on your way to your blessing. Joseph's spirit of excellence, humility, and work ethic were keys in getting Joseph promoted. It is not enough just to know that you are pregnant with purpose, you must still exercise your faith and be a good steward of the gifts and talents that God has given you; remember that success is when preparation meets opportunity. Joseph was prepared for each door of opportunity that God placed in his path.

Sometimes doctors have to verbally warn some pregnant women to stop gaining so much weight. Some women use their pregnancy as an excuse to just 'let themselves go'. They say; "Well I am eating for two!" The doctor has to correct them and inform them that they are actually eating for themselves, and the child is a recipient of what ever the mother eats, good or bad. Expectant mothers are encouraged to get involved in exercise classes and other health appropriate activities that are conducive for pregnant women. Joseph was pregnant with destiny and purpose; Joseph was bought as a slave but the Bibles states that Joseph was a very handsome and well built young man. Joseph refused to look like what he was going through. Joseph dressed himself not based upon his present circumstance, but based upon where God was taking him. Joseph exercised and took care of his physical being while he also nurtured and developed his spiritual, professional, and emotional self.

Lesson of Character

Genesis 39:6-9 (NLT); 6 So Potiphar gave Joseph
complete administrative responsibility over everything he
owned. With Joseph there, he didn't worry about a
thing—except what kind of food to eat! Joseph was a
very handsome and well-built young man, 7 and
Potiphar's wife soon began to look at him lustfully.
"Come and sleep with me," she demanded. 8 But Joseph
refused. "Look," he told her, "My master trusts me with
everything in his entire household. 9 No one here has
more authority than I do. He has held back nothing
from me except you, because you are his wife. How
could I do such a wicked thing? It would be a great sin
against God."

It has been said that character is who you truly are when you know no one else is looking. The Collegiate Hall of Fame coach John Wooden stated this about character; "Be more concerned with your character than your reputation, because your character is what you really are, while your reputation is merely what others think you are."

When Potiphar's wife attempted to have sex with him, Joseph refused to violate the sacred trust that Potiphar had placed in Joseph. Joseph understood that violating Potiphar's trust in him by sleeping with Potiphar's wife was the same as violating the trust and favor that God had given to Joseph. Even though Joseph was still technically an upper echelon slave in Potiphar's house, Joseph still remembered the sacred laws and tenets of God as written in the Ten Commandments. **Exodus 20:14 (NLT);** [14] "You must not commit adultery. **Exodus 20:17 (NLT);** [17] "You must not covet your neighbor's house. You must not covet your neighbor's wife, male or female servant, ox or donkey, or anything else that belongs to your neighbor."

Joseph refused to satisfy his sexual needs and those of Potiphar's wife at the expense of violating the sacred trust that both God and Potiphar had placed in Joseph. ***How can God trust you with a Destiny Kingdom, if God can not trust you with another person's spouse?***

Genesis 39:10-18 (NLT); [10] She kept putting pressure on Joseph day after day, but he refused to sleep with her, and he kept out of her way as much as possible. [11] One day, however, no one else was around when he went in to do his work. [12] She came and grabbed him by his cloak, demanding, "Come on, sleep with me!" Joseph tore himself away, but he left his cloak in her hand as he ran from the house. [13] When she saw that she was holding his cloak and he had fled, [14] she called out to her servants. Soon all the men came running. "Look!" she said. "My husband has brought this Hebrew slave here to make fools of us! He came into my room to rape me, but I screamed. [15] When he heard me scream, he ran outside and got away, but he left his cloak behind with me." [16] She kept the cloak with her until her husband came home. [17] Then she told him her story. "That Hebrew slave you've brought into our house tried to come in and fool around with me," she said. [18] "But when I screamed, he ran outside, leaving his cloak with me!"

The devil will not stop putting pressure on you to give in to the lusts of this world. Day after day Potiphar's wife kept putting pressure on Joseph to give in to his natural male desires, yet day after day Joseph chose to obey God and resist her sexual advances. One day when Potiphar's wife just could not take being rejected by her slave any longer, she attacked Joseph in an effort to entice him to sexual intercourse, Joseph ran from her and as a result of this ultimate rejection of her, she accused Joseph of attempted rape.

The evidence that Potiphar's wife used to accuse Joseph of rape, was the fact that she had the cloak or coat that Joseph wore as evidence that he had been close enough to her for her to grab it. This is the second time one of Joseph's coats or cloaks come into play in his destiny narrative. His brothers took and tore his first coat of many colors, and now Potiphar's lying wife is using

Joseph's coat as evidence against his character and integrity. The devil will use people to try and destroy you, by attempting to destroy what you believe about your true self and your destiny identity!

Genesis 39:19-23 (NLT); [19] Potiphar was furious when he heard his wife's story about how Joseph had treated her. [20] So he took Joseph and threw him into the prison where the king's prisoners were held, and there he remained. [21] But the LORD was with Joseph in the prison and showed him his faithful love. And the LORD made Joseph a favorite with the prison warden. [22] Before long, the warden put Joseph in charge of all the other prisoners and over everything that happened in the prison. [23] The warden had no more worries, because Joseph took care of everything. The LORD was with him and caused everything he did to succeed.

I am of the belief that if Potiphar, a seasoned soldier and captain of Pharoah's guard, had truly believed that Joseph had tried to rape his wife he would have killed Joseph on the spot. Potiphar knew his wife's adulterous proclivities and he knew the honesty and integrity of Joseph, this is why Joseph was not just placed in any prison, he was placed in the less cruel royal prison. Once again Joseph is receiving unfair treatment because he continued to refuse to allow someone else false expectations of him to break him.

The road to destiny will be filled with emotional highs and lows; Joseph was down when his brothers threw him into that dry well, he was down when he was sold into slavery, he was down while standing on the auction block waiting to be sold. Joseph was up when God placed him in Potiphar's house, he was up when Potiphar promoted him time after time. Joseph was down when Potiphar's wife harassed him, he was down when Potiphar's wife lied on him, he was down when he was demoted from Potiphar's house and placed into prison. Up and down, up and down, so goes the emotional roller coaster of life; life may take you up and down, but it is up to you to guard your emotions and your faith in God.

It is ok for life circumstances to go up and down, but don't allow life to take your faith up and down. You can not have an up and down faith; **James 1:2-8 (ASV);** [2] Count it all joy, my brethren, when ye fall into manifold temptations; [3] Knowing that the proving of your faith worketh patience. [4] And let patience have *its* perfect work, that ye may be perfect and entire, lacking in nothing.[5] But if any of you lacketh wisdom, let him ask of God, who giveth to all liberally and upbraideth not; and it shall be given him. [6] But let him ask in faith, nothing doubting: for he that doubteth is like the surge of the sea driven by the wind and tossed. [7] For let not that man think that he shall receive anything of the Lord; [8] a double minded man, unstable in all his ways.

No matter how bad of a hand life dealt Joseph, he never lost his faith in God's ability to guide him towards his destiny. Remember that nobody can stop you from transcending above the attacks of your enemies but you! Joseph is unjustly locked up in prison, but he still has God's favor on his life. The Bible says that Joseph prospered in prison and the Prison Warden had no worries while Joseph was in charge! Faith in God's anointing on your life is the only force that can give you the power to operate successfully under intense pressure. The Lord was with Joseph in everything that he did.

That Which Makes You Different, Makes You More Valuable

God will invent the circumstances needed in the earth in order for your gift to be revealed. That which makes you different, makes you more valuable. What is it that God has placed in your heart that is inching to get out? What idea, invention, book, song, poem, business are your pregnant with? What is it about you that cause people and even your family members to question you and call you strange? That which makes you unique, is the very thing that sets you apart! Don't run away from your 'unique you', because when God needs your unique gift you need to be ready to jump up off the bench of life and say; "Put me in God, I am ready (fully prepared) to play"!

It has been said, "every person is born a unique original and they end up dying a cheap copy". The dreams that

Joseph had made him different from his brothers; it was the God given dreams that Joseph had that caused his brothers to hate him and his father to question him. Dreaming got Joseph into trouble, and it is not by accident that God would use the subject of dreams to get Joseph out of trouble.

Genesis 40:1-19 (NLT); 1 Some time later, Pharaoh's
chief cup-bearer and chief baker offended their royal
master. 2 Pharaoh became angry with these two officials,
3 and he put them in the prison where Joseph was, in the
palace of the captain of the guard. 4 They remained in
prison for quite some time, and the captain of the guard
assigned them to Joseph, who looked after them. 5 While
they were in prison, Pharaoh's cup-bearer and baker each
had a dream one night, and each dream had its own
meaning. 6 When Joseph saw them the next morning, he
noticed that they both looked upset. 7 "Why do you look
so worried today?" he asked them. 8 And they replied,
"We both had dreams last night, but no one can tell us
what they mean." "Interpreting dreams is God's
business," Joseph replied. "Go ahead and tell me your
dreams." 9 So the chief cup-bearer told Joseph his dream
first. "In my dream," he said, "I saw a grapevine in front
of me. 10 The vine had three branches that began to bud
and blossom, and soon it produced clusters of ripe
grapes. 11 I was holding Pharaoh's wine cup in my hand,
so I took a cluster of grapes and squeezed the juice into
the cup. Then I placed the cup in Pharaoh's hand."
12 "This is what the dream means," Joseph said. "The

three branches represent three days. [13] Within three days Pharaoh will lift you up and restore you to your position as his chief cup-bearer. [14] And please remember me and do me a favor when things go well for you. Mention me to Pharaoh, so he might let me out of this place. [15] For I was kidnapped from my homeland, the land of the Hebrews, and now I'm here in prison, but I did nothing to deserve it." [16] When the chief baker saw that Joseph had given the first dream such a positive interpretation, he said to Joseph, "I had a dream, too. In my dream there were three baskets of white pastries stacked on my head. [17] The top basket contained all kinds of pastries for Pharaoh, but the birds came and ate them from the basket on my head." [18] "This is what the dream means," Joseph told him. "The three baskets also represent three days. [19] Three days from now Pharaoh will lift you up and impale your body on a pole. Then birds will come and peck away at your flesh."

What if Joseph had allowed the pain and hurt of his past to make him want to forget about ever dreaming again? Satan and his demons want you to be so traumatized, wounded and hurt from the pain of your past until you stop dreaming of a better life all together. Satan wants you to quit reaching for more, reaching for better, reaching for life. The very reason that Joseph was gifted enough to discern and explain the chief cup bearer's and chief baker's dreams rested in the fact that Joseph never stopped dreaming; nor did he stop nurturing and developing his God given gift of dreaming and interpreting dreams.

If Joseph had thrown away his God given gift because of the pain that it caused him in the past, he would not have had the 'dream keys' in his present circumstance to unlock the spiritual prison that had him bound. Joseph's interpretation of the dreams for Pharaoh's chief cup bearer and chief baker placed him in the company of Pharaoh's royal executive leadership team.

Don't Waste Your Waiting

Genesis 40:20-23 (NLT); 20 Pharaoh's birthday came
three days later, and he prepared a banquet for all his
officials and staff. He summoned his chief cup-bearer
and chief baker to join the other officials. 21 He then
restored the chief cup-bearer to his former position, so
he could again hand Pharaoh his cup. 22 But Pharaoh
impaled the chief baker, just as Joseph had predicted
when he interpreted his dream. 23 Pharaoh's chief cup-
bearer, however, forgot all about Joseph, never giving
him another thought.

The destiny of Pharaoh's chief cup-bearer and chief baker happened just like Joseph said it would happen. Pharaoh's cup-bearer promised to remember Joseph when he got out of prison and returned to Pharaoh's service, but just like most selfish people, when they get what they need from you, they forget about you.

The questions I hear most often from those who have been waiting a long time for God's promises to come to pass is this; "***When will God allow my water to break?*** When will God allow me to walk into my place of purpose and destiny? When will my ship come in?" My answer is this; while you are waiting on God to open doors, please don't waste your time while you are waiting. Use your 'waiting time' wisely. Professional athletes, professional back up singers, and professional Broadway performers get paid well to be prepared when their time comes. Don't waste your time whining, throwing a pity party crying look at poor me; use your waiting time to sharpen your skill, polish your gift, develop your character and up-grade your integrity, because when you are needed it will be show time and everyone will be able to tell if you are ready or if you are just faking it. Those who are caught faking performances will not be called back for a second act! Don't waste your waiting!

Faith Connects the 'Destiny Dots'

Genesis 41:1-15 (NLT); [1] Two full years later, Pharaoh dreamed that he was standing on the bank of the Nile River.[2] In his dream he saw seven fat, healthy cows come up out of the river and begin grazing in the marsh grass. [3] Then he saw seven more cows come up behind them from the Nile, but these were scrawny and thin. These cows stood beside the fat cows on the riverbank.

4 Then the scrawny, thin cows ate the seven healthy, fat
cows! At this point in the dream, Pharaoh woke up.
5 But he fell asleep again and had a second dream. This
time he saw seven heads of grain, plump and beautiful,
growing on a single stalk. 6 Then seven more heads of
grain appeared, but these were shriveled and withered by
the east wind. 7 And these thin heads swallowed up the
seven plump, well-formed heads! Then Pharaoh woke up
again and realized it was a dream. 8 The next morning
Pharaoh was very disturbed by the dreams. So he called
for all the magicians and wise men of Egypt. When
Pharaoh told them his dreams, not one of them could
tell him what they meant. 9 Finally, the king's chief cup-
bearer spoke up. "Today I have been reminded of my
failure," he told Pharaoh. 10 "Some time ago, you were
angry with the chief baker and me, and you imprisoned
us in the palace of the captain of the guard. 11 One night
the chief baker and I each had a dream, and each dream
had its own meaning. 12 There was a young Hebrew man
with us in the prison who was a slave of the captain of
the guard. We told him our dreams, and he told us what
each of our dreams meant. 13 And everything happened
just as he had predicted. I was restored to my position as
cup-bearer, and the chief baker was executed and
impaled on a pole." 14 Pharaoh sent for Joseph at once,
and he was quickly brought from the prison. After he
shaved and changed his clothes, he went in and stood
before Pharaoh. 15 Then Pharaoh said to Joseph, "I had
a dream last night, and no one here can tell me what it
means. But I have heard that when you hear about a

dream you can interpret it."

Two years had past and Joseph was still in prison, Pharaoh's cup-bearer had forgotten all about Joseph; and to Joseph, it may have felt like God had forgotten about him also. Thirteen years had passed since Joseph dreamed his dreams and it seemed that instead of his dreams taking him forward towards his purpose and upward towards destiny, instead it seemed that he was getting deeper and deeper into trouble; seemingly drifting farther and farther away from what his dreams had promised him.

While you are waiting on God to fulfill the promises concerning your life, please remember that God is not limited by time; God does not live by the time restraints of past, present, and future, God lives in what I term the **'Eternal Now'**; this means all the dots of existence are connected in the mind and will of God. "**Isaiah 46:9-10 (NLT);** [9] Remember the things I have done in the past. For I alone am God! I am God, and there is none like me.[10] Only I can tell you the future before it even happens. Everything I plan will come to pass, for I do whatever I wish". God knows how He has planned for the story to end before the first sentence is written; therefore you and I should have confidence in God's plan for our life. **Philippians 1:6 (NLT);** [6] And I am certain that God, who began the good work within you, will continue his work until it is finally finished on the day when Christ Jesus returns.

God causes Pharaoh, the god-king of Egypt, to have a dream regarding the earth-shattering famine that God was going to allow to happen. None of Pharaoh's wise men or magicians could interpret Pharaoh's dream because God had destined for Joseph to be the one to interpret this dream and witness to Pharaoh about the Hebrew God of Abraham, Isaac and Jacob. **Genesis 41:9-14 (HCSB);** [9] Then the chief cupbearer said to Pharaoh, "Today I remember my faults. [10] Pharaoh had been angry with his servants, and he put me and the chief baker in the custody of the captain of the guard. [11] He and I had dreams on the same night; each dream had its own meaning. [12] Now a young Hebrew, a slave of the captain of the guards, was with us there. We told him our dreams, he interpreted our dreams for us, and each had its own interpretation. [13] It turned out just the way he interpreted them to us: I was restored to my position, and the other man was hanged." [14] Then Pharaoh sent for Joseph, and they quickly brought him from the dungeon. He shaved, changed his clothes, and went to Pharaoh.

Pharaoh's fear of the dream he had and Joseph's ability to interpret dreams caused Pharaoh to release Joseph from jail suddenly. "**Proverbs 18:16 (NKJV);** [16] A man's gift makes room for him, And brings him before great men".

Once again it is not by accident that dreaming got Joseph into trouble and God would use Joseph's gift of dreaming to get him out of bondage. Joseph didn't sit on his gift concerning dreams; from the age of 17 years old to the age of 30 years old, Joseph has mastered the prophetic interpretation of dreams. Joseph didn't waste his waiting!

If Joseph had of allowed the trauma he experienced from his brothers because of his dream to cause him to hate dreaming, then Joseph would not have been prepared when Pharaoh called. Don't throw away your dreams because it is your dreams that point you in the direction of your destiny purpose. Success is when preparation meets opportunity! Stop looking at the calendar and your birth certificate and saying to yourself that you are too old; God's timing is perfect timing, therefore continue to get prepared for your water to break.

Genesis 41:15-16 (HCSB); 15 Pharaoh said to Joseph, "I have had a dream, and no one can interpret it. But I have heard it said about you that you can hear a dream and interpret it." 16 "I am not able to," Joseph answered Pharaoh. "It is God who will give Pharaoh a favorable answer."

- That which makes you different makes you valuable; Pharaoh understood that only Joseph could interpret the dream.

- Joseph didn't take the credit for the gift of dreams that God had given him. Joseph told

Pharaoh that it was God who gave Joseph the power to interpret dreams.

Genesis 41:28-36 (HCSB); 28 “It is just as I told
Pharaoh: God has shown Pharaoh what He is about to
do. 29 Seven years of great abundance are coming
throughout the land of Egypt. 30 After them, seven years
of famine will take place, and all the abundance in the
land of Egypt will be forgotten. The famine will
devastate the land. 31 The abundance in the land will not
be remembered because of the famine that follows it, for
the famine will be very severe. 32 Since the dream was
given twice to Pharaoh, it means that the matter has
been determined by God, and He will carry it out soon.
33 “So now, let Pharaoh look for a discerning and wise
man and set him over the land of Egypt.

- Pharaoh knows that his kingdom is in serious trouble because he knows that everything Joseph has said is true.

- Pharaoh knows that the problem his kingdom is about to encounter is beyond his skill set to solve. Pharaoh has enough humility and sensibility to look for someone to add to his executive team in order to solve the coming problem. Remember this; “You don’t get paid for what you know; you get paid for the problems you can solve”! Sharpen your anointing, gifts and skills in order to become a great problem solver. Destiny is always connected to problem solving.

Genesis 41:37-46 (NKJV); 37So the advice was good in
the eyes of Pharaoh and in the eyes of all his servants.
38 And Pharaoh said to his servants, "Can we find *such a
one* as this, a man in whom *is* the Spirit of God?" 39 Then
Pharaoh said to Joseph, "Inasmuch as God has shown
you all this, *there is* no one as discerning and wise as you.
40 You shall be over my house, and all my people shall be
ruled according to your word; only in regard to the
throne will I be greater than you." 41 And Pharaoh said to
Joseph, "See, I have set you over all the land of Egypt."
42 Then Pharaoh took his signet ring off his hand and put
it on Joseph's hand; and he clothed him in garments of
fine linen and put a gold chain around his neck. 43 And
he had him ride in the second chariot which he had; and
they cried out before him, "Bow the knee!" So he set
him over all the land of Egypt. 44 Pharaoh also said to
Joseph, "I *am* Pharaoh, and without your consent no
man may lift his hand or foot in all the land of Egypt."
45 And Pharaoh called Joseph's name Zaphnath-Paaneah.
And he gave him as a wife Asenath, the daughter of
Poti-Pherah priest of On. So Joseph went out over *all*
the land of Egypt. 46 Joseph was thirty years old when he
stood before Pharaoh king of Egypt. And Joseph went
out from the presence of Pharaoh, and went throughout
all the land of Egypt.

After 13 years of waiting, this is the day that Joseph's

water broke. After all of the troubles he had experienced, this was the day that Joseph got his breakthrough. Joseph woke up in prison that morning but on this night he would go to sleep in Pharaoh's palace. That morning, in prison, guards watched Joseph in order for him not to escape his jail cell, but on this night when Joseph laid down to sleep on royal sheets in the royal palace; now those royal guards would watch him to make sure he was protected.

Joseph's prophetic encounter interpreting Pharaoh's dream may have taken less than 20 minutes, but it took Joseph 13 years to get prepared for the 20 minutes encounter that changed his life. Don't waste your waiting; don't waste your waiting crying poor me; while you are waiting on God, be sure to get prepared for your destiny appointments. Confess the Word of God in your heart and your mouth! Speak life over yourself using Biblical faith building scriptures! Remember once again; success is when preparation meets opportunity.

When Joseph woke up in prison, on that morning he was a mere prisoner in Pharaoh's prison, but now Joseph is the Prime Minister/Vice-President of the Egyptian Kingdom. The dream that he told his brothers 13 years earlier had come to pass. Nobody believed in Joseph's dreams but Joseph. If no one else believes in your dreams, you just make sure you keep on believing in God's destiny plans for your life.

At 30 years of age Joseph becomes the second most

powerful man in the most powerful kingdom of that time. I suggest that each struggle that Joseph went through on his way to becoming Prime Minister / Vice-President of Egypt taught him something he would need when he was appointed to this destiny position. Let's connect the **destiny dots**;

1. Being hated by his brothers and betrayed by them prepared Joseph to deal with the deadly politics of Egypt. Joseph, a Hebrew, was frowned upon by other Egyptian power brokers because Joseph was an outsider, a prison who went from the prison to the palace and many Egyptian leaders were not pleased with this fact. No one would dare touch Joseph in Egypt because of Pharaoh's decree.

2. Being sold into slavery and working in Potiphar's house taught Joseph how to:
   - How to handle the business affairs of Egyptian royalty
   - How to understand the customs and rituals of Egypt
   - How to buy, sell and trade according to Egyptian law
   - How to make the best of bad conditions; remember that Joseph excelled and rose to leadership positions in Potiphar's house and in prison.

3. Resisting the seduction of Potiphar's wife taught Joseph how to resist the temptations of pagan

people, even to the point of being imprisoned. Joseph remembered that his power came from God and that he could not yield to all the temptations that pagan worship and idolatry offered him in Egypt.

4. Being in the royal prison with Pharaoh's royal cup bearer and royal baker provided Joseph with keen insight into the mind of Pharaoh, and the customs and rituals of Pharaoh's palace. Little did Joseph know that he would need this valuable information when God caused Pharaoh to call for Joseph. No one knew the protocol for dealing with Pharaoh better than the royal cup-bearer and royal baker. One wrong move, one wrong word, one wrong look could have literally meant that Pharaoh took Joseph's life. The Pharaohs of Egypt were considered gods on earth and they held absolute power. Joseph was risking his own life just by entering Pharaoh's presence.

If you find yourself becoming emotionally frustrated about the struggle you are experiencing on your road to destiny, remember Joseph and remember this; **Romans 8:28 (NKJV);** [28] And we know that all things work together for good to those who love God, to those who are the called according to *His* purpose.

The years passed and the famine hit Egypt and eventually reached the homeland where Joseph's father and brothers lived. These events ultimately led to

Joseph's brothers coming to Egypt looking for food and other resources to help them and their families survive the famine. Joseph's brothers had no idea that Joseph was still alive and they had never planned on seeing him again. As God would have it Joseph's brothers ended up in the presence of Joseph and they had no idea it was him. Joseph didn't look like what he had been through!

Genesis 45:1-5 (NKJV); 1 Then Joseph could not
restrain himself before all those who stood by him, and
he cried out, "Make everyone go out from me!" So no
one stood with him while Joseph made himself known
to his brothers. 2 And he wept aloud, and the Egyptians
and the house of Pharaoh heard *it.* 3 Then Joseph said to
his brothers, "I *am* Joseph; does my father still live?" But
his brothers could not answer him, for they were
dismayed in his presence. 4 And Joseph said to his
brothers, "Please come near to me." So they came near.
Then he said: **"I *am* Joseph** your brother, whom you
sold into Egypt. 5 But now, do not therefore be grieved
or angry with yourselves because you sold me here; for
God sent me before you to preserve life.

Joseph's brothers are in his presence after 13 years and Joseph wept out loud, Joseph cried uncontrollably. It is not strange that the Bible doesn't record Joseph crying when he was betrayed by his brothers, he doesn't cry when he is sold into slavery, he doesn't cry when he is lied on by Potiphar's wife and thrown into prison, he doesn't even cry when the royal cup-bearer forgets about him. Joseph only cries at the conclusion of his journey. Joseph's teaches us to stop crying over the small defeats we feel like we are encountering during our destiny journey, but cry tears of joy when you are standing in the victory circle.

Joseph said; "I am Joseph and God has added to me." This is what the name of Joseph means in the Hebrew language; God has added to me. Many people and situations tried to subtract from Joseph's life, they tried to prevent him from becoming who he was born to become. I am Joseph is not just a revealing to his brothers that he is the brother that they sold into slavery, when Joseph says 'I am Joseph', he is making a prophetic declaration that I have become who I was born to become. I am Joseph, **I have BECOME ME**, and in spite of everything I have been through I still became my 'destiny me'.

Genesis 50:18-21 (NKJV); 18 Then his brothers also went and fell down before his face, and they said, "Behold, we *are* your servants." 19 Joseph said to them, "Do not be afraid, for *am* I in the place of God? 20 **But as for you, you meant evil against me; *but* God meant it for good**, in order to bring it about as *it is* this day, to save many people alive. 21 Now therefore, do not be afraid; I will provide for you and your little ones." And he comforted them and spoke kindly to them.

The Hebrew word for meant is Chashab (khä·shav'), which means that God planned Joseph's life, God calculated every tough circumstance and obstacle that Joseph would encounter and God made a way for Joseph to survive and become. It also means that God invented the conditions that were necessary for Joseph to move into his destiny position.

God has planned and calculated the steps of those who trust in Him; *Psalm 37:23-25 (NKJV):* [23] The steps of a *good* man are ordered by the LORD, And He delights in his way. [24] Though he fall, he shall not be utterly cast down; For the LORD upholds *him with* His hand. [25] I have been young, and *now* am old; Yet I have not seen the righteous forsaken, Nor his descendants begging bread.

Each of the Pregnant Pauses that God allowed Joseph to experience had a God ordained purpose attached to it. From a Kierkegaardian perspective, God allowed Joseph's inner history (what was happening inside of Joseph) to supersede his outer history (what was happening to Joseph). Kierkegaard educates us that inner history engages the individual in a struggle with time. The struggle with time is the struggle to become and develop to the fullness of one's potential. The struggle within is connected to the element of time; you may ask when will my struggle be over? The struggles encountered during moments in time are struggles designed by God to bring the individual and moments in time together. God desires for outer history to happen to us in order for the inner history of faith to happen within us. God expects our outer circumstances to prompt an inner faith, therefore we begin to discover our authentic 'faith self'. These are the moments in time when we must exercise **our faith** in **God's plan** for our life.

The sum total of what has happened to you in life is described as the past, but this past can only be understood in relationship to what the future holds for you. Coming to know one's self involves connecting the destiny dots of your life with the moments in time you were required to exercise your faith. The patterns that begin to emerge in your struggle 'to become', forms a pattern of events that works together to shape your sense of whom you are and whose you are. The self who emerges from the events and moments of the past moves into the future by faith, a future that is shaped by past choices and divine destiny.

Joseph's struggle to become, as well as our struggle to become is a struggle not just with faith, but a struggle with time, because time places pressure on faith and causes us to ask; when will I arrive? We either want God to end the struggle we are in, or we want God to shorten the time of the struggle; our frustration with God is not over whether or not God has the power to do these things, but why won't He do it and do it now? Well the answer may be this, in the words of Kierkegaard; "To be born is to struggle and to struggle is to become"! There is no 'becoming' without struggle!

Joseph could boldly say; "I AM JOSEPH", after he had been through the proper amount of pruning, developing and struggles. Joseph didn't curse his struggles because he realized that the choices he made in the face of his external struggles helped to shape his inner person.

The struggles made Joseph wake up and realize that he was different, and it made him realize that he was alive for a reason and a purpose. Joseph had to remain alive because self awareness follows the awareness that one exists in time, and one has a God designed place and purpose in time. You must believe as Joseph believed; 'God will not waste my struggle'!

All of your struggles, trials and tribulations will finally make sense, when your water breaks and you give birth to the purposes of your destiny.

Made in the USA
Columbia, SC
31 October 2024

45270133R00086